Nine Steps to a Quality Research Paper

By Harry Stuurmans

Linworth
PUBLISHING, INC.

PROFESSIONAL GROWTH SERIES

Linworth Publishing, Inc.
Worthington, Ohio

Library of Congress Cataloging-in-Publication Data

Stuurmans, Harry
    Nine steps to a quality research paper / by Harry Stuurmans.
        p. cm. -- (Professional growth series)
    Includes index.
    ISBN 0-938865-35-8 (paperback)
    1. Report writing. 2. Research. I. Title. II. Series.
  LB1047.3.S78 1994
  371.3'028'12--dc20

94-13078
CIP

Published by Linworth Publishing, Inc.
480 East Wilson Bridge Road, Suite L
Worthington, Ohio 43085

Copyright © 1994 by Linworth Publishing, Inc.

Series Information:

    From The Professional Growth Series

ISBN 0-938865-35-8

5 4 3 2

Table of Contents

Step 6: Developing a Detailed Working Outline

Step 7: Writing the Rough Draft

Step 8: Revising the Rough Draft

Step 9: Preparing and Assembling the Final Copy

Acknowledgments

About the Author

Harry Stuurmans holds the A.B. in education from Calvin College in Grand Rapids, Michigan, and both the M.A. and Ed.D. in English language and literature from the University of Michigan in Ann Arbor. He also possesses a Standard Endorsement in Educational Media from Portland State University in Portland, Oregon. He has taught composition and literature at the secondary level and is currently the library media specialist at Fort Vancouver High School in Vancouver, Washington.

Linworth Publishing, Inc. would also like to thank the following school librarians and teachers for their contributions to *Nine Steps to a Quality Research Paper*:

Alice Evans Handy, Metcalf Jr. High School, Burnsville, Minnesota
Ron Marinucci, Milford High School, Milford, Michigan
Richard Soash, Shawnee Heights High School, Tecumseh, Kansas

To the Student:

So, you've been assigned to write something called a research paper. Maybe you've written research papers before. Maybe by now you are fairly comfortable with the process. If so, great! Your use for this work may be primarily as a reference.

On the other hand, maybe you've never done one of these things before. Or maybe you've done one, or even several, sort of, but you are still not completely comfortable with the assignment. You still feel a bit uneasy about the whole thing.

If so, help is on the way. This document is for you!

In this manual, the basic steps leading to the completion of a successful research paper, or term paper, as it is sometimes called, are clearly spelled out. Each of these steps is in turn broken down into easy-to-complete sub-steps, and in some cases, even into sub-sub-steps. Numerous examples are provided to help you make the transfer from theory to practice.

To make the document as easy as possible to use, symbols directing your attention to key concepts, recommended procedures, special tips, examples, and cautions are provided in the margins. These symbols and their meanings are as follows:

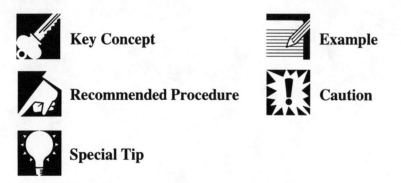

Key Concept **Example**

Recommended Procedure **Caution**

Special Tip

Finally, a word about how to approach an assignment like this.

Most students who feel frustrated or intimidated by the prospect of doing a research paper feel that way for one reason. Somehow they have never been able to get past viewing the assignment as one gigantic, complicated, overwhelming chore. They can only see this horrific monster staring them in the face, and it scares them half to death. What they fail to see is that this seemingly impossible task can easily be broken up into a series of small and relatively painless endeavors and that if they can just learn to tackle the job that way the monster quickly turns into a pussy cat. The assignment is not so difficult after all.

So, if you want to keep this project as simple as possible, remember this. Just take it one step at a time!

h.s.

To the Teacher:

Years of experience as an English teacher, and more recently as a library media specialist, have convinced me that student frustration with and frequent lack of enthusiasm for the research paper assignment has little to do with any inherent difficulty in the task itself and much to do with the failure or inability of students both to see the project as a process as well as a product and to manage their time for executing that process effectively.

You can help to do something about this.

First, stress to students the importance of approaching this assignment one step at a time. This not only means teaching the process chapter by chapter but collecting and providing feedback regarding student work each step of the way. It also means not allowing students to progress to a subsequent chapter until they have demonstrated the ability to produce what is called for in the previous one. Building on success is crucial to all good learning and highly important in this endeavor as well.

Second, encourage students to schedule their time for an assignment like this by outlining for them ahead of time, when the assignment is first made, just how much time they will have for each step and exactly what you expect when. This means publishing a detailed calendar, complete with due dates for the completion of individual steps along the way as well as a clearly specified due date for the final product. Stick to this calendar, and make sure students know from the outset that you expect them to meet the deadlines you have assigned.

In my observation, teachers who take these simple steps have happier, more successful students, and far more enjoyable papers to read!

h.s.

"What is written without effort is in general read without pleasure."
—Dr. Samuel Johnson, *Miscellanies*

Step 1
Selecting a Topic

1.1. What does it mean to select a topic?

To select a topic means to pick a subject to write about. It's that simple.

If your teacher has already done this for you, you may choose to ignore this chapter and proceed directly to Step 2: Narrowing the Topic. If your teacher is allowing you to pick your own subject, however, you will want to read this chapter carefully.

1.2. Why is selecting an appropriate research paper topic such an important step?

Remember when you were a little kid? Remember how you used to play with building blocks to see how high you could stack them? Remember how carefully you placed those bottom blocks in order to provide a solid foundation for the rest of your tower?

No doubt it's been years since you have even thought about playing with building blocks. In one very important respect, however, selecting the right topic for a research paper is a lot like laying those bottom blocks. In both cases you are setting the stage for something to come, and in both cases the care you give to setting that stage can have a tremendous impact on your success later on in the process.

Indeed, because constructing a successful research paper is such an intensely cumulative process—that is, because successful completion of the final steps is so dependent upon having laid a good foundation in the early stages—time spent at the outset laying such a foundation is time especially well spent.

Then, too, keep in mind that you are about to begin a project that will demand a considerable commitment of time and attention over the next several weeks. Doesn't it make sense to set yourself up for success by giving it that little bit of extra effort now?

1.3. How do I go about finding a topic that will be right for me?

1.3.1. Make a list of the possibilities.

You can choose from a number of processes to accomplish this first step. Some of the more productive ones are listed below.

As you work through these processes and as ideas come to mind, enter them on a word processor or jot them down on a blank piece of paper. Try to get down at least five or six potentially interesting topics, but remember that the longer your list the better your chance of identifying a subject that will really challenge your energy and imagination.

■ **Inventory your own special interests and curiosities.**

This suggestion may seem obvious, but take a little time to think about what you are really into. What would you especially like to learn more about? Are you a space freak? Have you been a baseball nut ever since you can remember? Are cars a passion with you? Have you always wondered what it would be like to live in an igloo?

Remember that almost any subject imaginable can make an appropriate topic for a research paper and that successful papers have been written on everything from candy bars to acupuncture, from the folly or wisdom of the modern-day monarchy to the life of the Roman slave. View the research paper project as an opportunity to explore a favorite subject in greater detail.

As you work through this process, be on the lookout for issues or areas of controversy related to your special interest. What do those who share your special interest disagree about? What gets them riled up? At the time of this writing, for example, the American and the National League still could not agree about the merits of the so-called "designated hitter" rule. Zero in on such areas of controversy because doing so will allow you to develop what is sometimes referred to as an "argumentative edge" in your paper—a spark that will go a long way toward increasing interest for both you and the reader.

■ **Browse magazines and newspapers.**

Spend some time looking through recent issues of a reputable newspaper (local or national) and magazines like *Time*, *Newsweek*, and *U.S. News & World Report*, which deal in a broad range of subjects. Scan the headlines and article titles for topics that pique your interest.

Once again, keep a lookout for subjects with at least a hint of controversy.

■ **Check special publications listing potential topics for research papers.**

Believe it or not, such publications actually exist. One of the best has long been published by the National Council of Teachers of English. At the time of this writing, its current title was *What Can I Write About? 7,000 Topics for High*

School Students. Ask your teacher or library media specialist for a copy of this booklet. If they do not have this particular title, perhaps they will be able to provide you with something similar.

■ **Seek out other, less formal, lists of potential topics.**

Ask your teacher and your library media specialist if they keep lists of topics that have worked for students in the past. Many of them do, and they will no doubt be happy to share them with you.

■ **Explore the basic subject indexes in your school or community library.**

All libraries, large and small, provide indexes to their book and magazine collections. No doubt you have had at least some experience using them by now. Libraries that maintain pamphlet files may also keep an index for this resource. The primary function of these indexes, whether in print or in electronic format, is to help library users tap into the broad range of resources available within the library. This makes them unusually comprehensive lists of potential research paper topics, covering as they do the entire range of subjects available.

Browse in these indexes a bit. While you are at it, ask your library media specialist to let you explore in the resources from which the subject headings for these indexes are actually taken—the *Sears List of Subject Headings* (no relation to the store in your local mall) and the *Library of Congress Subject Headings*. Because these are A to Z listings of subject headings, these titles can be convenient resources in which to spend a little time if you need reminders of the incredible range of possibilities out there.

1.3.2. Refine your list.

Once you have gathered a list of potential topics for your paper, select the two or three that most interest you—that most keenly arouse your curiosity. Remember that writing about a subject in which you are personally interested can make a tremendous difference in your attitude toward this assignment. Attitude is everything.

1.3.3. Check the availability of resources.

With your short list of potential topics in hand, spend some time in the library or libraries in which you plan to do most of your research to see if you'll be able to find the resources you need there.

■ **Check the indexes to the library's basic print collection.**

Begin by going back to the library's book and magazine indexes, whether they are automated (available on a computer) or in the traditional print format. Check subject headings as well as cross-references—headings that suggest other subjects under which you might look. If you are using computer indexes, take advantage of the power of key word searching as well. (If you are not sure what key word searching is, ask your teacher or library media specialist for help.) Note the number of titles listed that seem to have some relationship to the topics you are considering.

If the library in which you will be doing your research maintains a pamphlet file, ask to see an index to these files as well. Again, note the quantity and variety of material available on your two or three topics.

■ Browse in the reference collection.

Take time to look up your topics in a variety of encyclopedias, both general and specialized. (General encyclopedias are encyclopedias like the *World Book*, which attempt to provide at least some information about almost every subject imaginable. Specialized encyclopedias are encyclopedias like the *McGraw-Hill Encyclopedia of Science and Technology*, which limit their coverage to a specific subject or discipline and which therefore usually provide greater depth of information.) Note the degree of coverage these resources provide on your topic. Complete lack of coverage, or scanty coverage, may be an indication that information on your topic or topics may be harder to find than you would like.

■ Check into resources available in electronic or online format.

More and more libraries are making information available to their users electronically. Be sure to investigate your options in this area. If your library is making use of CD-ROM as an information storage and retrieval device, take the time to explore the software available. Likewise, if the library you are using has access to online searching via the Internet, for example, or through a database such as Dialog's *Classmate* program, make sure that you take advantage of these services. Once again, note the general availability of information relating to the topics you are considering for your project.

■ Talk with your school library media specialist and with the library staff at other libraries available to you.

Don't forget that your best friends and allies in the research process may well turn out to be the library media specialist or information specialist in your school's library media center and the staff of your local public library. Nobody knows the resources available to you better than these people, and you would be making a serious mistake not to take advantage of their knowledge and expertise. Share your short list of topics with them and ask for their advice regarding the availability of resources relating to them. They will be happy to help you, and a little time spent with them at this point could save you untold frustration and disappointment later as you proceed with this process.

1.3.4. Commit to a single topic.

Based on what you find out about the availability of information relating to
your limited list of potential topics and your own preferences for dealing with
them, make a commitment to a single topic. Write this topic neatly at the top of
a clean sheet of paper.

1.4. A word of caution:

As important as it is to take into account your own special interests and
curiosities in choosing a topic, remember that the assignment you are
undertaking has been designed, at least in part, to help you master a *process*.
This process will be enough of a challenge without the additional burden of
finding material for a topic that is so arcane or far out that no one has written
very much about it. Accordingly, unless you have access to sophisticated
information retrieval systems, whether in your school library media center or in
nearby public or academic libraries, you will do well to avoid highly
specialized subjects. In other words, think twice before tackling topics such as
"Recent Medical Breakthroughs in the Treatment of Bone Cancer" or "The
Poetry of Mao Zedong."

<u>Notes</u>

Step 2
Narrowing the Topic

2.1. What does it mean to *narrow* the topic?

To narrow a topic is to reduce it in size, to place limits on it, to focus it. It is to take a large subject like baseball, for example, and whittle it down to something manageable like the designated hitter rule, or to take a subject like drug abuse and reduce it to something like steroid use among Olympic athletes.

In either case, a topic about which volumes could be and undoubtedly have been written has been reduced in size to something that might be treated successfully in a paper of 10 to 15 pages.

2.2. Why is narrowing the topic so important?

The obvious requirements of time (usually a few short weeks) and space (typically no more than 10 or 15 pages) make it important that you focus on a relatively specific issue or problem. In other words, you don't have forever to do this project, and you are not going to write a book.

Let's take another look at the subject of drug abuse. If you were to tackle this subject in this unrestricted form, without trying to narrow it or to limit it in any way, you would need to cover an immense amount of material. You would have to research the entire history of drug abuse—and not just in our own country but throughout the world. You would have to deal not simply with causes but also with effects and treatments—and not just for one drug but for all drugs. Of course, it would no doubt also be a good idea to say something about trafficking in illicit drugs and efforts to control such trafficking. And then there is the issue of decriminalization. And on, and on, and on.

Taking notes for such a broad topic would be an absolute nightmare. You would have to write down everything that has ever been written on the subject of drug abuse—and a great deal has been written on it.

In fact, so much has been written about drug abuse that you would not be able to say anything specific in a short paper. Indeed, rather than saying more about less (going into greater detail about a smaller topic), which is usually what makes writing interesting, you would be forced to say less about more. You would have to deal in the broadest of generalities just to cover the subject. There would be no time or space to talk about particulars, no time to describe specific instances, examples, situations, no time to give your paper the color and immediacy that makes a reader sit up and take notice.

In short, unless an effort is made to place some limits on a subject such as drug abuse, doing a paper on it could be a very big project indeed, and no doubt an exceedingly frustrating one as well.

2.3. How do I go about narrowing my topic?

2.3.1. Try dividing and subdividing it yourself.

One way to narrow a topic is simply to start chopping away at it. Brainstorm a bit about the topic to see how it can be divided and subdivided to the point where it begins to represent something you might realistically be expected to tackle in a research paper of moderate length.

Let's go back to the topic of drug abuse. Suppose that instead of taking on the entire subject of drug abuse, we decided to deal only with drug abuse *among athletes*. With this single step we have placed a major limitation on the population with which we need to be concerned in our treatment of the subject of drug abuse. Generally speaking, we can forget about the need to deal with the question of drug abuse as a major cause of blight in our inner cities, or with drug abuse as a significant problem among high school students, or even with the threat of drug abuse to the unborn. If we do choose to deal with such things as the causes of drug abuse or trafficking in illegal drugs or decriminalization, we will be able to do so with a much narrower focus.

Now, suppose that we were to take the process a step further. Suppose that we elected to deal only with drug abuse among *Olympic* athletes. Having done so, we could suddenly afford to ignore the entire subject of drug abuse among professional athletes, among college athletes, even among high school athletes. Instead, we could focus on drug abuse among a very select group of people— athletes who participate in the Olympic games.

Finally, suppose we took this process one more step. Suppose that we decided to deal only with *steroid* abuse among Olympic athletes. By taking this step we could eliminate the problem of having to deal with the use and abuse by Olympic athletes of everything from crack to cocaine, from heroin to LSD. Instead, we could zero in on the abuse of one drug only—anabolic steroids.

In three simple steps we have moved from a huge, overwhelming topic, drug abuse, which could never be successfully treated in a student research paper of moderate length, to a very manageable topic—steroid abuse among Olympic athletes, a topic which a student has at least a fighting chance of treating successfully in a paper of 10 to 15 pages.

Just to review, the process went something like this:

Initial topic:	Drug abuse
First cut:	Drug abuse among athletes
Second cut:	Drug abuse among Olympic athletes
Third cut:	Steroid abuse among Olympic athletes

2.3.2. Find out how others writing about your subject have divided it.

This can be done in a couple of ways. One is to locate a book that deals broadly with your subject. Examine the table of contents and note chapter headings. Occasionally chapters themselves will be subdivided. Note these subdivisions and follow the author's lead in zeroing in.

Or look up your subject in a good encyclopedia, either in print or electronic format, and note how it has been divided and subdivided there. (Incidentally, this works especially well if you are writing about a country or about a state or province within a country.) For example, a recent edition of the *World Book*, known as *Information Finder* in its electronic format, subdivides the entry for Canada as follows:

> The Nation
> People
> Way of Life
> The Arts
> The Land
> Climate
> Economy

Each of these sections is further subdivided. The section on "The Arts," for example, is broken down as follows:

> Literature
> Painting and Sculpture
> Theater
> Music
> Ballet and Opera
> Motion Pictures
> Architecture

Following the lead of an encyclopedia this way, it is easy to move quickly from a large and totally unsuitable topic, like Canada, to something much more manageable, like Canadian popular music or the Stratford Shakespearean Festival.

2.3.3. Check to see how professional indexers have divided your subject.

Magazine indexes work especially well for this, again whether in print or electronic format. A check of a recent issue of EBSCO's *Magazine Article Summaries* on CD-ROM, an online periodical index, shows no fewer than 57 subheadings listed under the subject of "Abortion," including the following:

> Corrupt Practices
> Economic Aspects

Government Policy
Laws & Legislation
Physiological Aspects
Political Aspects
Psychological Aspects
Public Opinion
Religious Aspects
Social Aspects

Needless to say, although further narrowing would probably still be in order, beginning to work with any one of the above as it relates to the subject of abortion would have obvious advantages over trying to take on the subject in its entirety.

To cite a second example, the *Readers' Guide to Periodical Literature*, a long-standing print index to periodicals, not only shows several basic entries relating to the subject of basketball—"Basketball, Professional"; "Basketball, College"—but it typically subdivides these rather broad headings still further, as in the case of "Basketball, College," which it breaks down as follows:

Accidents and Injuries
Betting
Ethical Aspects
Organization and Administration
Recruiting
Television Broadcasting
Schedules
Tournaments

Indeed, it is not uncommon for the *Readers' Guide to Periodical Literature* to list more than 100 subdivisions for a subject—as it does, for instance, for the subject of computers—and to carry the process even a step further by subdividing the subdivisions.

2.4. A few reminders:

Do not expect to complete the process of limiting your topic before you have even begun your research. Keep in mind that limiting the topic is often an ongoing process which is complete only when your paper itself is complete. As you continue your research and your writing, you will become increasingly aware of just how much you can take on without overextending yourself.

Remember also that just as a topic can be too broad, a topic can also be too narrow; and that although it is almost always advisable to say more about less, it is possible to overdo it. In narrowing your topic, try to find that middle ground. You will make things much easier for yourself down the road.

Step 3
Formulating a Preliminary Question Outline and a Tentative Thesis

3.1. What is a preliminary question outline?

A preliminary question outline is nothing more than a list of questions to which you hope to find answers in your research.

It is "preliminary" in the sense that it is not final—in the sense that it can still be changed as you learn more about your subject. It is called an *outline* because, even though it may lack the numbering system and the subordination one customarily associates with an outline, it does represent the initial step in establishing a plan for your paper.

3.2. Why do I need a preliminary question outline?

Before you can begin looking for information on your topic, you must have a *focused* idea regarding the information you are seeking. You simply cannot cover everything. A preliminary question outline helps to provide such focus. By knowing exactly what the questions are you want to answer, you can avoid wasting a lot of time trying to take notes on everything relating to your topic— even though you may have done a good job of narrowing it.

Second, just as any problem is easier to solve once it has been broken down into smaller parts, so too is gathering information for a research paper much easier if you can identify the eventual subparts of your paper right from the start. The preliminary question outline helps you to do this by making it easier for you to begin thinking of your paper as a collection of clearly identifiable sections and subsections rather than as some overwhelming, ill-defined, "too-big-even-to-think-about" mass.

3.3. How do I go about formulating a preliminary question outline?

3.3.1. Begin by doing a little brainstorming.

On a word processor or on a clean piece of paper list as many questions as you can bring to mind relating to your topic. Because this is a brainstorming activity, it might be a good idea to ask a friend to help you. However you do it, do not worry too much about how the questions relate to each other or about order or even about quality. Simply try to get down as many questions as possible. Indeed, the only caution here might be to avoid questions that can be answered with a simple *yes* or *no*, since such questions tend not to "go anywhere" once they have been answered. (Actually, such questions can usually be transformed into *why* or *how* questions.)

For example, suppose that you have selected "Steroid Use Among Olympic Athletes" as a subject for a paper. You might list questions such as the following:

1. How widespread has been the use of steroids at recent Olympic games?
2. Is the problem getting better or worse?
3. When did the problem begin?
4. How long has the use of steroids been a problem at the Olympics?
5. Why have some Olympic athletes been tempted to use steroids?
6. Which Olympic events have been most apt to involve the use of steroids?
7. What steps has the International Olympic Committee taken to discourage the use of steroids at the Olympic games?
8. How successful have these steps been?
9. What are the penalties for using steroids in Olympic competition?
10. How does the International Olympic Committee test for the use of steroids during the games?
11. What are steroids?
12. What are the short-term side effects of using steroids?
13. What are the long-term side effects of using steroids?
14. Who are some of the more famous Olympic athletes who have been found guilty of using steroids?
15. What does the future hold?

3.3.2. Consolidate your questions.

Once you feel that you have pretty much exhausted the questions relating to your topic, examine them carefully to see if some of them might not be closely related or even overlapping or identical. (Are you really asking the same question in more than one way?) Whenever possible, combine such questions to eliminate duplication. This will allow you to reduce your total number of questions and consolidate your research. In the list above, for example, you might decide that questions 3 and 4 are really asking the same thing, as are questions 7 and 9. Likewise, you might decide that if questions 1, 3, and 4 are successfully answered, question 2 will be unnecessary. Finally, you might conclude that question 14 will probably get covered if question 6 is properly treated and that question 10 will likely receive sufficient treatment if questions 7 and 9 are successfully combined and answered.

At this point you should also take a hard look at your questions to see if you may have included some that you would really rather not tackle in this particular project. Among the questions listed above, for example, you may decide that questions 12 and 13 on the short and long-term effects of anabolic steroids, while interesting and undoubtedly related to your primary topic, are not your primary topic and might actually be better left to another paper altogether. Accordingly, you might wish to eliminate them from your list. In short, regard this as still another opportunity to place limits on your research. Do not be afraid to take advantage of it.

At any rate, by thus combining like questions and by eliminating irrelevant and unwanted ones, a list that once included 15 questions can be substantially reduced:

1. How widespread has been the use of steroids at recent Olympic games?
2. How long has the use of steroids been a problem at the Olympics?
3. Why have some Olympic athletes been tempted to use steroids?
4. Which Olympic events have been most likely to involve the use of steroids?
5. What steps has the International Olympic Committee taken to discourage the use of steroids at the Olympic Games?
6. How successful have these steps been?
7. What are steroids?
8. What does the future hold?

3.3.3. Organize your questions.

With your reduced and consolidated list before you—it might consist of as few as three or four questions—attempt to organize the remaining questions into whatever order seems most logical. In doing so, try to anticipate which questions will ultimately need to be answered first (in composing your paper, not in doing your research) before you can go on to deal with others. In the list above, for example, a workable sequence might be as follows:

1. What are steroids?
2. Why have some Olympic athletes been tempted to use steroids?
3. Which Olympic events have been most apt to involve the use of steroids?
4. How long has the use of steroids been a problem at the Olympics?
5. How widespread has been the use of steroids at recent Olympic Games?
6. What steps have the International Olympic Committee taken to discourage the use of steroids at the Olympic Games?
7. How successful have these steps been?
8. What does the future hold?

3.4. What is a tentative thesis?

A tentative thesis is a single declarative sentence—a sentence that makes a statement—in which one attempts to summarize the point or points one hopes to make in a paper. It is "tentative" in the same sense that an outline at this stage is preliminary. It is subject to change as the work progresses.

3.5. Why is it important to have a tentative thesis?

A tentative thesis is important to the student about to begin a research project for much the same reason that a working hypothesis is important to the laboratory scientist about to begin an experiment. Together with the preliminary question outline, it helps to provide *focus* for the task at hand. It suggests a destination; it makes it easier to hold one's thoughts and ideas together; it establishes a framework for the entire effort. It says, "This is where I am going; this is the point, or these are the points, that I hope to make; this is what this paper is going to be about."

3.6. How do I go about formulating a tentative thesis?

3.6.1. Anticipate your conclusion or conclusions.

Once you have completed the preliminary question outline, take some time to guess at the answers to the questions you have posed for your research. What information do you *expect* your research will uncover relative to these questions? What do you think you will find? What conclusion or conclusions do you anticipate reaching?

To do this, of course, takes a bit of bravery. You don't really know exactly what you will discover in your research. But that's okay. Take a stab at it anyway. Go out on a limb. If the scientist can take the time to establish a working hypothesis before undertaking an experiment, you can do as much before beginning your research, and with a similar result. You will be assured of a basic focus for your research.

3.6.2. Formulate your anticipated conclusion or conclusions into a single declarative sentence.

After taking some time to guess at the conclusion or conclusions you expect to reach in your paper, attempt to put that conclusion or those conclusions into a single declarative sentence—a sentence that makes a statement. (Questions do not make appropriate thesis statements.) This sentence will become your tentative thesis.

For a topic such as steroid use among Olympic athletes, one might try something like the following:

```
Tentative Thesis: The use of anabolic steroids by Olympic
                  athletes has been occurring for a long
                  time, but steps taken in recent years by
                  the International Olympic Committee have
                  greatly reduced the problem.
```

3.6.3. Position your thesis sentence where you will not be able to ignore it.

When you have managed to reduce the conclusion or conclusions that you expect to reach in the course of doing your research to a single, declarative sentence, write or place this sentence above your preliminary question outline.

This sentence, this tentative thesis, together with your preliminary question outline, should be like a beacon to you as you begin the task of gathering information on your subject. If you use them as they are intended to be used, if you keep your sights focused squarely upon them throughout your research, you can be sure of writing a satisfactory paper with a minimum of wasted effort.

3.7. Something to keep in mind:

The outline and the thesis you compose at this point are preliminary and tentative. You may very well revise or expand them before you have finished your research. Do not allow them to limit your research. They are not cast in stone. In other words, if in doing your research it becomes obvious that you have overlooked an important aspect of your subject, do not hesitate to add a question or questions. By the same token, if your research makes it apparent that some of your questions are really of little importance or that you have bitten off more than you can chew, do not be afraid to discard some of them.

<u>Notes</u>

Step 4
Assembling a Working Bibliography

4.1. What is a working bibliography?

A working bibliography is a list of sources related to or potentially useful in researching your chosen topic—a list of materials that hold promise for helping you find answers to the questions posed in your preliminary question outline.

It is called a *working* bibliography to distinguish it from the *final* or *formal* bibliography, which will appear at the end of the paper you eventually submit to your instructor.

4.2. Why do I need a working bibliography?

Long ago somebody figured out that a division of labor could lead to greater efficiency and productivity. Hence the assembly line in many factories. Of course, writing a research paper, which is essentially an individual effort, is not exactly like building an automobile or putting together a television set, in which cases different people do different jobs. Nevertheless, the concept of doing one task at a time can help you greatly with the kind of project you are now undertaking, particularly at this stage in the process.

Imagine, for example, how inefficient it would be to go to the card or online catalog, locate information about a single book relating to your topic, copy down or print that information, leave the catalog, locate the book, check it out if need be, carry it to a desk or table, jot down the information you will need for your bibliography or source card, take notes from the book, and then turn right around and repeat the whole operation—over and over and over. Think of how many times you would have to find the subject in the catalog. Think of how many trips you would have to make to the book shelves, to the circulation desk, and so on.

Wouldn't it be simpler and make a lot more sense to make one trip to the catalog, copy down in one or two sittings the information you need to locate all the books the library has on your subject, and then be through with the library's book index for good? Think of the time you would save, to say nothing of the steps you would eliminate by not having to move back and forth from catalog to shelves to circulation desk to table to catalog again.

4.3. How do I go about creating a working bibliography?

4.3.1. Gather the necessary materials.

Computer software designed to help students store, manipulate, and retrieve bibliographic information is now being marketed. Until this software becomes more widely available, however, and until computers themselves become even more portable and accessible than they currently are, most of you will probably still need to do this job the "old-fashioned" way—with pen or pencil and a plentiful supply of index cards.

Index cards have traditionally been used for compiling working bibliographies because they make it easy to add and delete from a list and because they can be readily alphabetized—an advantage you will appreciate when you are ready to compile your final bibliography.

Unless your teacher has specified a particular size, the size of index card you use is largely up to you. Many students prefer the 4 x 6 inch size because it gives them plenty of room on which to get down all the necessary information without squeezing anything.

Whatever you do, *do not make the mistake of trying to use notebook paper for this task*—even if you have the best of intentions for transferring the information to index cards later. At the very least, you will end up wasting a lot of time in making the transfer. At worst you will greatly increase the odds of miscopying important information.

4.3.2. Think about where you might find the information you need.

Once you have gathered the supplies you will need to make a list of potential resources, take a few minutes to think about the questions you have posed for yourself in your preliminary question outline. What kind of information will you need to answer these questions and where will that information most likely appear? In books? In magazines and newspapers? In pamphlets? In some electronic media? Remember that books generally do a better job of treating historical subjects or subjects that have at least been making the news for a couple of years. Magazines, newspapers, and online databases, on the other hand, tend to do a better job of providing information on current events and news items.

Actually, you may wish to spend a little time at this point discussing your topic once again with your school library media specialist or with the staff at whatever other libraries may be available to you. Not only will they be able to suggest which types of media will be of most help to you, but they will also be able to alert you to resources that may not be so immediately obvious or that may be unique to their collections.

4.3.3. Search the indexes.

Once you have decided which types of resources hold the greatest promise for helping you answer the questions in your preliminary question outline, seek out the appropriate indexing mechanisms. For books and other resources in the library's "permanent" collection you will undoubtedly wish to do some exploring in the catalog—whether in traditional print format or in an automated version. For leads on magazine and newspaper articles you will want to take advantage of whatever periodical indexes are available to you—again, whether in print or in electronic format. If the library you are using maintains a file of pamphlets and clippings, you may wish to consult whatever indexing mechanism is available for such material. If your library subscribes to the *Social Issues Resources Series* materials or to similar resources, you will want to check the cross reference guides for these items. If you have access to online information services, you may wish to examine whatever indexes or thesauruses accompany these services.

4.3.4. Copy down the necessary bibliographic information.

As you come across titles that suggest a connection to your subject or the potential for answering one or more of the questions listed in your preliminary question outline, jot down the bibliographic information for that item—one citation per card. For a book with a single author—probably the simplest kind of resource to cite—this bibliographic information typically includes the following:

> The author's name
> The title of the book (and edition, if given)
> The name of the city in which the book was published
> The name of the publisher
> The date of publication
> > (See the sample bibliography cards.)

The bibliographic information you will need to cite for other kinds of resources varies considerably, however, and you will want to pay close attention to the examples given, both to make sure that you are including everything you should be including and that you are getting down the information in a sequence that will make it easy later on to draft notes and bibliographic citations in the format recommended by the Modern Language Association, the format generally recognized as the standard in this field and the format followed throughout this guide.

Note that the examples given below are in a *line-by-line* format as opposed to the *paragraph* format you will eventually use in your formal bibliography. They have been given this way for two reasons: (1) Copying down the various parts of the so-called bibliographic information on the separate lines of a note card makes it easier to focus on the specific pieces of information needed as opposed to the exact *format* in which that information will eventually need to be rendered—an important consideration at this stage of the process. (2) Allowing a separate line for each piece of bibliographic information makes it possible to indicate, by leaving a line blank, that information was missing from the indexing used and will still need to be filled in once the source is in hand for note taking.

Having said all this, it should also be pointed out that there is no law saying your bibliographic or source cards must be done in a line-by-line format. If you would prefer to copy down the bibliographic information for your sources in the same paragraph format that you will eventually use in your final bibliography, simply turn to Step 8 and follow the examples given there for formal bibliographic citations.

4.4. Sample bibliography cards:

4.4.1. Nonreference books:

a. A book written by a single author:

Information you will need:

Name of library in which the item may be found (may be abbreviated)
Call number

Author's name (last name first)
Title of book (underlined), edition (if given)
Place of publication (first American city listed)
Publisher
Date of publication

Example:

```
FVHS LMC
362.2/Dol

Dolan, Edward F.
Drugs in Sports, Rev. ed.
New York
Franklin Watts
1992
```

b. A book written by two or three authors:

Information you will need:

Name of library in which the item may be found (may be abbreviated)
Call number

First author's name (last name first), and second author's name (first name first)
or, for three authors
First author's name (last name first), second author's name (first name first), and third author's name (first name first)
Title of book (underlined), edition (if given)
Place of publication (first American city listed)
Publisher
Date of publication

Example:

```
FVHS LMC
363.7/McC


     McCuen, Gary E., and Ronald P. Swanson
     Toxic Nightmare: Ecocide in the USSR &
          Eastern Europe
     Hudson, WI
     Gary E. McCuen
     1993
```

Example:

```
FVHS LMC
952/Col


     Collcutt, Martin, Marius Jansen, and
          Isao Kumakura
     Cultural Atlas of Japan
     New York
     Facts on File
     1988
```

c. A book written by more than three authors:

Information you will need:

Name of library in which the item may be found (may be abbreviated)
Call number

First author's name (last name first), followed by *et al.* (Latin for *and others*)
Title of book (underlined), edition (if given)
Place of publication (first American city listed)
Publisher
Date of publication

Example:

```
FVHS LMC
011/Nin


     Barron, Neil, et al.
     1990 What Do I Read Next? A Reader's
          Guide to Current Genre Fiction
     Detroit
     Gale
     1991
```

d. A book authored by a corporation, commission, association, or committee:

Information you will need:

Name of library in which the item may be found (may be abbreviated)
Call number

Name of the corporation, commission, association, or
    committee responsible for the work
Title of book (underlined), edition (if given)
Place of publication (first American city listed)
Publisher
Date of publication

Example:

```
FVHS LMC
330.9/Wor

     The World Bank
     World Development Report 1993
     New York
     Oxford UP
     1993
```

e. A book authored by a government body or agency:

*Information
you will
need:*

Name of library in which the item may be found (may be abbreviated)
Call number

Name of nation, state, or other governing body
sponsoring the publication
Name of specific agency responsible for authorship
Name of sub-agency or sub-agencies (if given)
Title of book (underlined), edition (if given)
Place of publication
Publisher
Date of publication

Example:

```
FVHS LMC
317.97/Was


        Washington State
        Office of Financial Management
        Forecasting Division
        Washington State 1993 Data Book
        Olympia
        Washington State Department of Printing
        1993
```

Example:

```
FVHS LMC
317.3/Uni


        United States
        Department of Commerce
        Economics and Statistics Administration
        Bureau of the Census
        Statistical Abstract of the United
              States 1992, 122nd ed.
        Washington
        GPO
        1992
```

f. A book with an editor or compiler instead of an author:

*Information
you will
need:*

Name of library in which the item may be found (may be abbreviated)
Call number

Name of editor or compiler (last name first), followed by *ed.* or
  comp. (whichever applies)
Title of book (underlined), edition (if given)
Place of publication (first American city listed)
Publisher
Date of publication

Example:

```
FVHS LMC
960/Afr

     Martin, Phyllis M., and Patrick
          O'Meara,eds.
     Africa, 2nd ed.
     Bloomington
     Indiana UP
     1986
```

g. A book that has been republished (such as a classic novel re-issued in paperback):

Information you will need:

Name of library in which the item may be found (may be abbreviated)
Call number

Author's name (last name first)
Title of book (underlined)
Date of original publication
Place of republication (first American city listed)
Publisher
Date of republication

Example:

```
FVHS LMC
F/Cle

     Twain, Mark
     The Adventures of Huckleberry Finn
     1884
     Topeka
     Econo-Clad
     1985
```

h. A selection from an anthology or collection:

Information you will need:

Name of library in which the item may be found (may be abbreviated)
Call number

Author of specific selection (last name first)
Title of the specific selection (in quotation marks)
Title of the book in which the selection appears (underlined),
Edition (if given)
Editor of book (regular order, preceded by *Ed.*)
Place of publication (first American city listed)
Publisher
Date of publication
Pages number or numbers on which the individual selection
appears

Example:

```
FVHS LMC
SC/Oxf


Poe, Edgar Allan
"The Tell-Tale Heart"
The Oxford Book of American Short
     Stories
Ed. Joyce Carol Oates
New York
Oxford UP
1992
91-96
```

4.4.2. Reference books:

a. An article or entry from a general encyclopedia (such as *World Book*, *Americana*, or *Britannica*):

Information you will need:

Name of library in which the item may be found (may be abbreviated)
Call number

Author's name (if given; last name first)
Title of article or entry (in quotation marks)
Name of encyclopedia (underlined)
Edition (date or number, followed by *ed.*)
Date of publication (if not part of edition statement)

Example:

```
FVHS LMC
R/031/Wor


          Faulk, Odie B.
          "Western Frontier Life"
          The World Book Encyclopedia
          1993 ed.
```

b. An article or entry from a *single-volume* reference work:

*Information
you will
need:*

Name of library in which the item may be found (may be abbreviated)
Call number

Author of article or entry (if given; last name first)
Title of article or entry (in quotation marks)
Title of the book in which the article or entry appears
    (underlined), edition (if given)
Editor of book (if given; regular order, preceded by *Ed.*)
Place of publication (first American city listed)
Publisher
Date of publication
Page number or numbers on which article or entry appears

Example:

```
FVHS LMC
R/973.03/Rea


    Gordon, John Steele
    "Iron and Steel Industry"
    The Reader's Companion to American
        History
    Eds. Eric Foner and John A. Garraty
    Boston
    Houghton Mifflin
    1991
    574-75
```

c. An article or entry from a *multivolume* reference work (volumes *not* individually titled):

Information you will need:

Name of library in which the item may be found (may be abbreviated)
Call number

Author of article or entry (if given; last name first)
Title of article or entry (in quotation marks)
Title of the book in which the article or entry appears (underlined), edition (if given)
Editor of work (regular order, preceded by *Gen. ed.*)
Specific volume number in which article or entry appears (preceded by *Vol.*)
Place of publication (first American city listed)
Publisher
Date of publication
Page number or numbers on which article or entry appears
Number of volumes in set (followed by *vols.*)

Example:

```
FVHS LMC
R/301/Enc


    Weil, Frederick D.
    "Political Party Systems"
    Encyclopedia of Sociology
    Gen eds. Edgar F. Borgatta and Marie
        L. Borgatta
    Vol. 3
    New York
    Macmillan
    1992
    1485-92
    4 vols.
```

d. An article or entry from a *multivolume* reference work (each volume *individually* titled):

Information you will need:

Name of library in which the item may be found (may be abbreviated)
Call number

Author of article or entry (if given; last name first)
Title of article or entry (in quotation marks)
Title of the volume in which the article or entry appears (underlined)
Editor of specific volume (if given; first name first, preceded by *Ed.*) volume number of specific volume cited, followed by title of entire set, edition (if given)
Place of publication (first American city listed)
Publisher
Date of publication
Page number or numbers on which article or entry appears
Number of volumes in entire set (followed by vols.)
General editor of set (if given; first name first, preceded by *Gen. ed.*)
Inclusive publication dates for all volumes

Example:

```
FVHS LMC
R/305/Enc


Sutton, Susan Buck
"Greeks"
Encyclopedia of World Cultures: Europe
Ed. Linda A. Bennett
Vol. 4 of Encyclopedia of World Cultures
Boston
G. K. Hall
1992
131-34
10 vols.
Gen. ed. David Levinson
1991-95
```

4.4.3. Periodical material:

a. An article or story from a newspaper:

*Information
you will
need:*

Name of library in which the item may be found (may be abbreviated)
Call number or special location in the library

Author of article (if given; last name first)
Title of article (in quotation marks)
Name of newspaper (underlined)
Date of issue
Edition (if unique)
Section and page number or numbers

Example:

```
FVHS LMC
Periodical Collection

     Millbank, Dana
     "Little Luxemberg Sees a Big Problem"
     The Wall Street Journal
     31 March 1994
     Western ed.
     A11
```

b. An article or story from a magazine:

Information you will need:

Name of library in which the item may be found (may be abbreviated)
Call number or special location in the library

Author's name (if given; last name first)
Title of article (in quotation marks)
Title of magazine (underlined)
Date of issue (month and year only for monthly publications)
Page number or numbers

Example:

```
FVHS LMC
Periodical Collection

     Lemonick, Michael D.
     "Too Few Fish in the Sea"
     Time
     4 April 1994
     70-71
```

c. An article or story from a scholarly journal:

*Information
you will
need:*

Name of library in which the item may be found (may be abbreviated)
Call number or special location in the library

Author's name (if given; last name first)
Title of article (in quotation marks)
Title of journal (underlined)
Volume number and issue number, e.g., 10.4 (omit issue
number if pagination is continuous from one issue
to the next)
Year of publication (in parenthesis)
Page number or numbers

Example:

```
FVHS LMC
Periodical Collection

    Carpenter, Ted Galen
    "Closing the Nuclear Umbrella"
    Foreign Affairs
    73.2
    (1994)
    9-13
```

4.4.4. Reprinted material:

a. Previously published articles appearing in collections and anthologies (such as *Social Issues Resources Series* or *Opposing Viewpoints*):

Information you will need:

Name of library in which the item may be found (may be abbreviated)
Call number or special location in the library

Author of article (if given; last name first)
Title of article as it appeared in the original source (in quotation marks)
Title of original source (underlined)
Date of original publication
Section and page number or numbers in original publication, if given (section number unnecessary if original was not a newspaper)
If reprinted under original title, the words *Rpt. in* followed by the title of the work in which the reprint appears (and volume number if a SIRS item); if reprinted under a new title, the words *Rpt. as* followed by the new title and the title of the work in which the reprint appears
Place of publication (first American city listed)
Publisher
Date of publication
Article number for SIRS items; page number or numbers for non-SIRS items

Example:

```
FVHS LMC
Reserve Shelf

     Longman, Jere
     "From Soweto, It's a Hard Run to
          Glory"
     Philadelphia Inquirer
     14 June 1992
     A1+
     Rpt. in Sports Vol. 4
     Boca Raton
     Social Issues Resources Series
     1993
     Art. 34
```

Example:

```
FVHS LMC
327.1/Nuc

        Weiss, Leonard
        "Tighten Up on Nuclear Cheaters"
        Bulletin of the Atomic Scientists
        May 1991
        Rpt. as "The International Atomic
            Energy Agency is Ineffective"
        Nuclear Proliferation: Opposing
            Viewpoints
        San Diego
        Greenhaven
        1992
        73-78
```

4.4.5. Nonprint material:

a. A lecture:

Information you will need:	Lecturer's name (last name first)
	Title of lecture (in quotation marks)
	Location of lecture
	City and state in which lecture was given
	Date on which lecture was given

Example:

```
Barber, David
"The United States and Pacific Rim Trade"
Fort Vancouver High School Contempory
World Problems Class
Vancouver WA
28 March 1994
```

b. A television or radio program:

Information
you will
need

Name of program (underlined if a single program; in quotation
marks if part of a series)
Narrator's name (if given; first name first)
Name of writer and producer (if given; first name(s) first)
Name of series (if program is part of a series; underlined)
General program title (if available)
Station name and location
Date

Example:

```
"What Is Money Anyway?"
Narr. Christopher Castile
Writ. and prod. Jane Paley and Larry Price
Step by Step, Money Made Easy: The ABC
        Kids' Guide to Dollars and Sense
ABC Saturday Special
KATU, Portland, OR
2 April 1994
```

c. A personal interview:

Information
you will
need:

Name of person interviewed (last name first)
Type of interview
Date of interview

Example:

```
Peterson, Donald L.
Personal interview
1 April 1994
```

4.4.6. Computer-accessed material:

a. Computer software:

Information
you will
need:

Name of library in which the item may be found (may be abbreviated)
Call number or special location in the library

Author of program (if given; last name first)
Name of program (underlined)
The version (if given)
The designation *Computer software*
Publisher
Date of publication
Disk operating system and version (if given)
Size of program, form of program (if given)

Example:

```
FVHS LMC
Electronic Information Center

    PC Globe
    Vers. 4.0
    Computer software
    PC Globe
    1990
    MS DOS 2.0+
    512KB, disk
```

b. CD-ROM software:

*Information
you will
need:*

Name of library in which service may be obtained (may be abbreviated)
Special location in the library

Give all the information you would for ordinary printed
material (author, title, publisher or publication, date)
Version (if given)
The designation *Computer software*
Publisher
Date of publication
Disk operating system and version (if given)
The designation *CD-ROM*

Example:

```
FVHS LMC
Electronic Information Center

    Ford, John K. B.
    "Whale"
    Information Finder
    Vers. 2.4
    Computer software
    World Book
    1993
    MS-DOS 3.1+
    CD-ROM
```

c. Material from online information services (such as *BRS* or *Dialog*):

Information you will need:

Name of library in which service may be obtained (may be abbreviated)
Special location in the library

Give all the information you would for ordinary printed material (author, title, publisher or publication, date)
Vendor name
File number and item number (if available)

Example:

```
FVHS LMC
Dialog Online Search Center

   Reuters, Sharon Robb
   "U.S. Coaches Credit China's Rapid Rise
        to 'Pharmaceutical Warfare'"
   Seattle Times
   5 December 1993
   Weekend ed.
   C12
   Dialog
   File 707 item 07339158
```

d. Material from online news services (such as *X-Press*):

Information you will need:

Name of library in which service may be obtained (may be abbreviated)
Special location in the library

Author's name (if given; last name first)
Title or headline of story (in quotation marks)
Name of news service or information provider (if given)
City from which story was filed (if given)
Date story was received
Name of service (e.g., X-Press Information Services)
Time stamp (hour: minute: second)

Example:

```
FVHS LMC
X-Press Online Search Center

"Clinton Pitches Health Plan"
Associated Press
Troy, NC
5 April 1994
X-Press Information Services
15:35:33
```

If you do not find a sample above that matches the resource you are using, ask your teacher or library media specialist for help. If they cannot help you, perhaps they will be able to refer you to a recent edition of one of the following commonly used guides to documentation. The examples above follow the *MLA Handbook*. The others may recommend a slightly different format. All of them will at least be able to give you some idea regarding what bibliographic information is needed to provide adequate documentation:

Campbell, William Giles, Stephen Vaughan Ballou, and Carole Slade. *Form and Style: Theses, Reports, Terms Papers*. Boston: Houghton Mifflin.
The Chicago Manual of Style. Chicago: The University of Chicago Press.
Gibaldi, Joseph, and Walter S. Achtert. *MLA Handbook for Writers of Research Papers*. New York: Modern Language Association of America.
Turabian, Kate L. *A Manual for Writers of Term Papers, Theses, and Dissertations*. Chicago: The University of Chicago Press.

Remember, however, that no guide can furnish examples for every situation imaginable and that it is frequently necessary in drafting a working bibliography to exercise a bit of personal ingenuity in combining various models and examples. In this activity a dash of common sense and a willingness to adapt can be a big help.

4.5. Things to keep in mind:

■ Be careful to write or print legibly. Having to go back later to verify a smudged word or illegible date is time-consuming and frustrating. (To guarantee legibility, use a pen, or at the very least, a good pencil with a sharp point.)

■ Make bibliography cards even for sources that seem only marginally related to your subject. Titles can be deceiving. Some sources will turn out to have a greater bearing on your subject than you may at first think. Remember also that it is much easier to discard a bibliography card that turns out to be a dud than it is to keep going back to a library's catalog and indexes for new material.

■ Make sure that as you make your bibliography cards you are careful to get down all the information that you will need for your final bibliography. If the indexing you are using omits certain information (place of publication for a book perhaps), be sure to leave room on your card for including this information when you actually get the source in hand.

■ If, even after a careful examination of the source itself, you are unable to locate the information needed to fill a specific line or position on your bibliography card, simply leave that line or position blank. (You will find specific instructions on how to deal with such omissions in the steps dealing with documentation.)

Step 5
Taking Notes

5.1. What does it mean to take notes?

To take notes is to gather bits, pieces, and sometimes whole chunks of information from the sources listed in your working bibliography that look as though they may help you to answer the questions you have posed for your research in your preliminary question outline. These notes may be *summaries*, *paraphrases* (information you have put into you own words), or *direct quotations*. (More about this later.) They have traditionally been made on index cards to allow you to arrange and rearrange them as you organize your paper.

5.2. Why should I bother to take notes?

Some of you may have gotten by until now without ever having actually taken notes, at least not in the formal or traditional sense. You have managed to survive so-called "research paper" assignments by working directly from the source material (frequently a general encyclopedia or perhaps a very limited number of books or magazines) to the end product—your paper. You took a bit of information from here, a bit from there, mixed it together, tossed in a prayer for good luck, and hoped that somehow it would all add up to something when you were finished. (Sound familiar?)

This "process" may have worked, sort of, for short written reports, even if your teachers called them "research papers." Even those of you who have survived with it so far, however, have probably sensed its basic inadequacies.

For one thing, moving directly from the source material to your paper is a cumbersome way to bring together related information from different sources.

Then, too, students who try to get by using this method have to do a lot of skipping around in their source material. ("Let's see now. Wasn't there some information relating to this point in that book I just had?") This skipping around not only means handling each source several times but wasting considerable time within each source trying to locate information that you know is there but that is just not at the tips of your fingers any more. ("Was it on page 65 or 72? Was it at the top of the page or at the bottom?")

Finally, working directly from the source material to the paper tends to impose artificial organizational patterns on a paper because the urge to follow wherever a source leads is difficult for some students to resist. The result is often a paper that is really little more than a linking together of one summarized article or chapter after another.

Using a formal note-taking process eliminates such problems. Because all the notes from one source are taken at one time (or in a couple of sittings at most), materials can be returned to the library following the completion of the note-taking process and never consulted again. Since the information is written down, it does not get lost. And since different pieces of information are put on different cards, it is easy to add, delete, rearrange, and group like information together. Finally, the organizational pattern can be one of your own choosing, not one imposed upon you by whatever article or book you happen to be working from at the moment.

5.3. How do I get started taking notes?

5.3.1. Gather the necessary materials.

Computer software already exists that will undoubtedly change forever the way students take notes. If you have access to such technology, consider yourself very fortunate, and by all means take advantage of it. It should make your task much easier and give you vastly improved access to and control over your material once you have gathered it. Once again, however, until this technology becomes much more widely available than it currently is, most of you will still need to take notes by hand on index cards. In either case, you will want to have your working bibliography, your preliminary question outline, and your tentative thesis readily available to you as you undertake this task.

5.3.2. Review your preliminary question outline.

Before you even attempt to locate your first source, take a minute to re-examine the questions in your preliminary question outline. Remember that these are the questions for which you are seeking answers in your research. You will want to keep them very much on your mind. In fact, it is a good idea to keep your preliminary question outline physically in front of you the whole time that you are taking notes. Doing so will help to keep your attention focused where it should be and greatly reduce the temptation to take notes you do not need.

5.3.3. Locate and retrieve the first source listed in your working bibliography.

This should be easy since all the information you will need to find the material (the library in which it can be found, the call number, etc.) is already there in the upper left-hand corner of your bibliography or source cards. Let the librarian know if you need help in finding your sources.

5.3.4. Double check the information on your bibliography card.

Once you have the source material in hand, take a minute to make sure that the information on your bibliography card is accurate and complete. Are your spellings correct? Do you need to add an author's name? Is there more to the title than was indicated in the index you used? Make corrections as needed and fill in any gaps that may exist.

5.3.5. Verify the source's currency and relevance to your needs.

Is the material sufficiently up-to-date? Whether the resources from which you are taking notes were written in the mid-fifties or within the last year or two may not be important if you are writing about medieval architecture, but it could be very significant indeed if your topic happens to be something like the atmosphere on Mars or DNA replication, where new discoveries are being reported almost monthly.

If currency seems important for your topic, take the time to check the publication dates on your resources. This information for magazines and newspapers is typically up front and obvious. In books the copyright date is usually found on the verso, the page immediately behind the title page. The publication dates of other resources can usually be found with a bit of effort. Be skeptical of resources for which no date can be found.

Equally important, is the source really dealing with your subject? If you are working with a book, the table of contents and the index can usually help you answer this question. In other resources you may have to rely on headings and subheadings. In some cases you may have to skim a bit to get a good idea about a source's relevance to your topic.

5.3.6. Look for the big picture.

If you are satisfied that the material does indeed meet the requirements of currency and relevance, take some time to skim those sections of the work that seem most closely related to your topic. (If you are dealing with a magazine or newspaper article or with a short pamphlet, you will undoubtedly want to examine the entire document.) Before you even think about taking your first note, however, try to get a feel for the writer's scope, orientation, and organizational scheme. This will help you to avoid quoting out of context or otherwise misrepresenting the material with which you are dealing.

5.3.7. Zero in on the answers to your questions.

Once you feel comfortable with the material in hand, begin a serious search for information that will help you answer the questions you have posed for yourself in your preliminary question outline. Check indexes and tables of contents to find what you need. When you come across something that seems to answer one of your questions, make a note containing that information.

5.4. Should I summarize, paraphrase, or quote directly?

You have three choices of format in which to take your notes. You can summarize, you can paraphrase, or you can quote directly. Each has its place in the note-taking process. Which format you decide to use will depend on the material being noted and the time you have in which to write it.

5.4.1. Summarizing:

To summarize means to reduce the material you are noting to its basic essentials, to take from a larger body of information only those bits and pieces that you really need. Think of summaries as that pure concentrate or extract with which you are left after you have squeezed out everything that is not absolutely critical.

Summarize if you need only the most basic facts or ideas from the material you are researching.

Example of a summary

Original passage:

> To see just how stringent the Olympic testing program is, we need only look at the procedures used in the 1984 and 1988 games. In both years an Olympics representative was assigned to each event. Immediately after any event, the representative summoned the first-, second-, and third-place winners, along with another competitor picked at random. They were escorted to a nearby drug-testing station, or, as it was widely called, a doping control station. There each athlete gave two samples of urine.
>
> One sample was stored away under strict security in case it would be needed later. The second went to a laboratory maintained by the International Olympic Committee, there to be tested. If the test proved negative—if no forbidden substance revealed itself—all was well. But if the result came up positive, a medical committee immediately informed the athlete and his or her team officials of the finding.
>
> A second analysis was then carried out in the presence of International Olympic Committee representatives and officials from the athlete's team. If it, too, proved positive, the athlete was stripped of his or her medals.*

* Edward F. Dolan, <u>Drugs in Sports</u>, rev. ed. (New York: Franklin Watts, 1992) 127.

A summary:

> In the 1994 and 1988 games the top three performers in each event and one participant selected randomly were required to provide two urine samples immediately following competition. One sample was tested for banned substances; the

other was set aside as a backup. If the first sample tested positive, the second was tested in the presence of representatives from the IOC and from the athlete's team. If both tests proved positive, the athlete was forced to give up any medals he or she might have won.

5.4.2. Paraphrasing:

To paraphrase means to put something into your own words—*really into your own words*. It means coming to a thorough understanding of what someone is trying to say and internalizing it so thoroughly that you can look away from the source and restate the idea or information in words and phrases that are completely your own. *It does not mean simply rearranging another's words a bit here and a bit there or leaving out a few words now and then and trying to pass off this slightly reconstructed material as your own.* (See the example below of an *unacceptable* paraphrase.)

Paraphrase when you need the information you are noting in its entirety but not exactly as expressed in the source. Do not paraphrase if the wording of the material you are noting is more *concise*, more *vivid*, or more *colorful* than your paraphrase could be, if the material you are noting is unduly lengthy and would benefit from reduction (see summarizing above), or if you do not have time to do a good paraphrase.

Examples of paraphrasing

Original passage:

   The new USOC guidelines call for testing of any athletes likely to qualify for international competition (including alternates), as well as one-fifth of the remaining participants in all events. The testing is to take place immediately following the competition, and a testing official is present during every phase of the testing. Two separate specimens are collected from each athlete. In the event of a positive test, the second specimen is analyzed as an automatic appeal on the athlete's behalf. Any athlete who does not cooperate or refuses to be tested is disqualified.*

   * Jeff Meer, <u>Drugs and Sports</u> (New York: Chelsea House, 1987) 100-01.

An *unacceptable* paraphrase:

   The latest <u>USOC guidelines</u> involve testing all athletes <u>likely to qualify for</u> the national team and a <u>fifth of the remaining participants</u>. (100) The testing occurs <u>immediately following the competition</u> in the presence of an official. Athletes are required to submit <u>two separate specimens</u>. If the first sample tests positive, the second is submitted for a similar analysis <u>as an automatic appeal on the athlete's behalf</u>. Those <u>who do not cooperate or refuse to be tested</u> are automatically <u>disqualified</u>. (101)

Notice how closely the "paraphrase" parallels the original in vocabulary and phrasing. Notice how often little pieces of direct quotation (the words and phrases underlined) creep into the "paraphrase." Such a "paraphrase" is not paraphrase at all but a brutalized quotation, without benefit of quotation marks.

An *acceptable* paraphrase:

```
     The USOC currently tests all those favored to make the
national team and 20 percent of the other athletes
attempting to qualify. (100) Directly after the completion
of each event, and in the presence of an official, athletes
are required to submit a pair of urine samples. If the first
sample tests positive, the second is routinely submitted for
a similar analysis. Athletes who fail to participate fully
and willingly in this process are by definition ineligible
for team membership. (101)
```

5.4.3. Quoting directly:

To quote directly means to copy down an author's exact words, word for word.

Quote directly if the material you are noting is expressed in a such a way that summarizing it or putting it into your own words would seriously weaken its impact or effect, or if summarizing it or putting it into your own words would consume more time than you are prepared to invest at this point in the process.

If you do quote, keep in mind the following:

- Be sure you get down the *exact* words used, including errors in spelling or punctuation that may appear in the original. Such errors should be followed in brackets by the word *sic*, which is Latin for *thus*, indicating that the error is in the original and not in your copying.
- Be sure to indicate clearly that you are quoting. In other words, use appropriate quotation marks.
- Use double quotation marks—"'single marks within double ones'"— around material you are quoting that is already enclosed in quotation marks.
- Use ellipsis marks (. . .) and brackets [ ] to indicate omissions and insertions, respectively.

If you find it desirable to quote several passages from a single source, or if the passage you are quoting is long, consider printing or photocopying the material in question, using a scissors to cut out the passage or passages you need, and attaching them to your note cards with clear tape or a little glue.

Example of a direct quotation

Original passage:

> ...In addition to a compulsive personality, many hard-driving competitors develop what is called the "athletic mind-set."
>
> The term springs from the fact that athletes train hard for a single goal or a series of goals. Perhaps the single goal is an Olympic gold medal. Perhaps the series of goals adds up to a string of victories that carry the individual from local to national and then international competitions—or to the ranks of the professionals. Soon, it's all too easy for the athletes to think of nothing else. Put yourself in their place and you might imagine yourself saying, "I must get to where I'm going—at any cost."*

> * Edward F. Dolan, <u>Drugs in Sports</u>, rev. ed. (New York: Franklin Watts, 1992) 50.

A direct quotation:

> "The term ['athletic mind-set'] springs from the fact that athletes train hard for a single goal or a series of goals. Perhaps the single goal is an Olympic gold medal. Perhaps the series of goals adds up to a string of victories that carry the individual from local to national and then international competitions—or to the ranks of the professionals. Soon, it's all too easy for the athletes to think of nothing else."

5.5. What should I include on the note card?

5.5.1. A "slug"

- The slug is a short phrase that summarizes the contents of the note. You might think of it as a headline for your note.
- The slug should be one word if possible, or at least short enough so that it does not become a note in itself. (If your slug takes more than one line at the top of your note card, it is too long.)
- The slug should be descriptive enough so that you are not forced to reread the entire note each time you wish to consider it for use.
- The slug should be situated in the upper left-hand corner of the index card so that it is the first thing you see when you glance at the card.

5.5.2. The note itself

- The note may be a *summary*, a *paraphrase* (something you put into your own words), or a *direct quotation*. (See above.)
- The note should be limited to one basic fact, one closely related group of facts, one idea, one opinion, one anecdote, or one example.
- The note should be kept short. (If your notes consistently run over one card in length, you are not following the advice given just above.)

Place your note in the middle section of the index card, skipping at least one line between the slug and the note.

If your note does not fit on one card, use a second card. Label this card exactly the same as the first, with the same slug, bibliographic link, and page number. Then label your first card **1** and your second card **2**.

5.5.3. A link to the bibliography card

The link to the bibliography or source card, or citation, should be the very first piece of bibliographic information on that card—usually an author's last name.

For unsigned material, use a shortened form of the title.

If you have multiple bibliography cards for different works by the same author, follow the author's last name with a shortened version of the appropriate title.

The link to the bibliography card should appear beneath the note and slightly off to the right. If there is room on the note card, skip at least one line between the note and the bibliographic link.

5.5.4. A reference to the pages from which the note was taken

If the note is from more than one page, include beginning and ending page numbers. Make it clear in the note itself what part of the note comes from which page. (See the sample paraphrase note card below.) The reference to the page number or numbers should come immediately after the link to the bibliography or source card, usually an author's last name.

5.6. Sample note cards

5.6.1. A summary:

Slug or phrase summarizing content of note —— Testing procedures at the '84 & '88 games

In the 1984 and 1988 games the top three performers in each event and one participant selected randomly were required to provide two urine samples immediately following competition. One sample was tested for banned substances; the other was set aside as a backup. If the first sample tested positive, the second was tested in the presence of representatives from both the IOC and from the athlete's team. If both test proved positive, the athlete was forced to give up any medals he or she might have won. — *The note itself*

Dolan 127 — *Page from which note was taken*

Bibliographic link–in this case the author's last name

5.6.2. A paraphrase:

Slug or phrase summarizing content of note

```
Current USOC testing procedures

The USOC currently tests all those favored to
make the national team and twenty percent of
the other athletes attempting to qualify. (100)
Directly after the completion of each event,
and in the presence of an official, athletes
are required to submit a pair of urine samples.
If the first sample tests positive, the second
is routinely submitted for a similar analysis.
Athletes who fail to participate fully and
willingly in this process are by definition
ineligible for team membership. (101)

                                      Meer 100-101
```

The note itself

Page numbers inserted to show what part of the note came from what page

Page from which note was taken

Bibliographic link–in this case the author's last name

5.6.3. A direct quotation:

Slug or phrase summarizing content of note

```
"Athletic mind-set" a motive for using
steroids

"The term ['athletic mind-set'] springs from
the fact that athletes train hard for a
single goal or a series of goals. Perhaps the
single goal is an Olympic gold medal. Perhaps
the series of goals adds up to a string of
victories that carry the individual from
local to national and then international
competitions-or to the ranks of the
professionals. Soon, it's all to easy for the
athletes to think of nothing else."

                                      Dolan 50
```

The note itself

Brackets used to indicate inserted material

Page from which note was taken

Bibliographic link–in this case the author's last name

5.7. A warning about plagiarism:

The word *plagiarism* (verb form: *to plagiarize*) has its roots in the Latin word *plagium*, which means, quite literally, man-stealing or kidnapping. Over the centuries, the word has developed a slightly different but closely related meaning. Today it is most frequently used in the world of arts and letters, and it means to try to pass off someone else's words and ideas as one's own What we are talking about here is nothing less than literary theft, and it constitutes a serious offense.

Plagiarism can take various forms. The most obvious and most flagrant involves taking what someone else has written and inserting it word for word into one's own writing without giving the reader any clue (quotation marks, documentation) that the material has been borrowed from someone else.

A second less blatant but equally serious form of plagiarism involves taking a phrase, a sentence, or a passage from another writer and re-arranging the words just enough so that your writing is no longer a word-for-word quotation and then inserting the re-arranged material into your own writing without benefit of quotation marks or other documentation. Sound familiar? Student writers are famous for this kind of plagiarism. Unfortunately, this practice is still plagiarism, still literary theft. (See the previous example of an *unacceptable* paraphrase.)

A third form of plagiarism involves taking thoughts and ideas from another's writing and inserting these thoughts or ideas into one's own writing as though they were one's own, without any form of acknowledgment. Although this is perhaps a more subtle form of stealing, thoughts and ideas are no less intellectual property than word-for-word quotations; and borrowing them from someone else's writing without proper acknowledgment is still stealing, still "kidnapping," and still wrong.

Plagiarism is frequently a problem for student writers, sometimes because they do not understand that what they are doing is stealing and therefore wrong, and sometimes because they simply have not learned to summarize or paraphrase very well. As you begin the process of taking notes, and later on as you incorporate your notes into your paper, be careful how you handle the words and ideas of others. Be fair both with your reader and with those whose ideas and information you are using.

5.8. Other things to keep in mind:

- If you are taking notes by hand, *avoid the temptation to write on the back of a note card.* You want to be able to see what is on your note cards at all times. What is on the back is out of sight, out of mind.

- *Be accurate and thorough.* A bit of care taken now can save you immense amounts of time later. When you are struggling to crank out your rough draft, the last thing you need is to be making a return trip to the library to track down one of your sources again because you were careless about getting that quote exactly right or because you forgot to record a page number.

Step 6
Developing a Detailed Working Outline

6.1. What is meant by a detailed working outline?

As the third step in the research paper process, you developed a preliminary question outline—a list of questions to which you hoped to find answers in your research. In doing so, you took the initial step in establishing a plan for your paper.

Since then you have built a working bibliography and taken the notes that will provide you with much of the content for your paper. Before actually writing your paper, however, you must return to the planning process begun in your preliminary question outline. You must develop a detailed working outline.

A detailed working outline is a skeletal plan showing in more depth than was possible (or even desirable) in the preliminary question outline exactly what points you expect to make in your paper and the order in which you expect to make them. You might think of it as an elaborate road map that will chart the course for the development and support of your thesis statement. (More on that subject in a bit.)

It is called a *working* outline not only because it is the outline from which you will work as you put together the first draft or rough draft of your paper but because it represents your best effort at this stage in the process to organize the material you have gathered in your research. (As you may have learned from other writing experiences, drafting a paper is often a fluid process; and exactly how everything fits together is sometimes not entirely clear until one has wrestled with the very act of composition itself.)

6.2. Why is it important to have a detailed working outline?

No self-respecting builder would think of starting to work on a simple house, let alone a modern 40-story office building, without access to a complete set of blueprints. Nor does the smart traveler set off on a lengthy automobile journey without first spending some time with an atlas or a good set of road maps, carefully plotting the trip to make sure that he or she will reach the desired destination efficiently and enjoyably, without wasting precious fuel and valuable time.

Your objectives in successfully completing the research paper are not unlike the builder's or the traveler's. You too have something to build. You too have a destination to reach. To accomplish your objective, however, you need a blueprint, a map, a plan.

As was suggested above, you have the beginning of such a plan in your preliminary question outline. If you were careful in constructing it, it has no doubt been most useful in guiding your research and in helping you to begin seeing your paper in terms of its parts. As useful as it may have been for you up to this point, however, it is not really up to the task of providing the kind of detailed guidance you will need to write the first draft of your paper, any more than simply knowing how many bedrooms belong in a house would give a builder adequate guidance in framing the structure, or any more than simply knowing the names of the cities one wants to visit would properly prepare a traveler for an automobile trip.

In short, you need an outline that goes into considerably more detail than your preliminary question outline. You need a plan that shows not only where the walls go but even where the light switches must be placed, not only what roads you need to take but exactly where the turns are and precisely how many miles it is from point A to point B. You need a plan that describes not just the major points you hope to make in your paper but that outlines what subpoints and even sub-subpoints you will need to make to support and develop those major points.

6.3. How do I go about developing a detailed working outline?

6.3.1. Develop a "slug" outline.

Creating a detailed working outline is typically a three-step process. The first step involves developing what is commonly known as a slug outline, an outline composed essentially of the slugs from your note cards.

To create a slug outline begin by finding yourself a large surface upon which to work. A good-sized table top is great. If one is not available, try using the floor. On the table top (or on the floor) sort your note cards into piles, grouping together cards with similar slugs. For example, if you were writing a paper on steroid abuse among Olympic athletes and you had one note card with the slug "Most experts believe steroids increase muscle mass and body weight" and another with the slug "Steroids are thought to increase strength and endurance," you would probably want to group the two cards together since they both deal with a common subject, the impact steroids are commonly thought to have on the user.

When you have sorted all of your cards, give each pile a general heading. In other words, *make slugs for the slugs*. In the case of the example above, for instance, you might want to try grouping the two cards under a heading such as "How steroids affect the athletes who take them." (If some groups consist of only one card, use the slug from that card as the heading for that group. See numbers 3, 5, and 17 below.)

On separate note cards, copy down these headings or "super slugs," listing under each one the slugs for the individual cards in the group.

Once you have your note cards organized this way, take another look at your preliminary question outline. Have you managed to find sufficient material to answer all the questions you posed for your research at the outset? If you have not, and if the questions still seem important, you may wish to return to the library to seek additional information.

When you are satisfied that you have the material you need to address the questions listed in your preliminary question outline thoroughly and with confidence, arrange the new cards you have made—the ones with the slugs from your individual note cards grouped under what we are now calling "super slugs"—into whatever order seems most logical. (Your preliminary question outline should be a big help here.)

Finally, copy the entire result onto a clean sheet of paper or enter it on a word processor. The final product might look something like the example below:

Sample slug outline:

1. Basic facts about steroids
       Origin and initial use of steroids
       What steroids are
       Definitions of <u>androgenic</u> and <u>anabolic</u>

2. What steroids supposedly do for athletes
       Most experts believe steroids increase muscle mass
           and body weight
       Steroids are thought to increase strength and
           endurance
       Steroids may increase aggressiveness and hostility

3. Some athletes feel they need steroids just to compete

4. Desire to win a strong motive for Olympic athletes to use
    steroids
       Desire to win almost obsessive among some athletes
       Dr. Goldman's research on desire to win
       Dr. Mirkin's question reveals overwhelming desire to win

5. Greed an important factor in some Olympians' use of steroids

6. Pressure from entire world of sports pushes athletes to
    do "whatever is necessary"
       Pressure comes from peers and teammates
       Coaches sometimes encourage athletes to use drugs
       Fans expect athletes to win at all costs

7. Steroid use among Olympic weightlifters
    Olympic weightlifters generally thought to be first to use
    Olympic weightlifters believed to be among biggest abusers
    Problem so bad among weightlifters some think sport
        should be eliminated

8. Other Olympic events involved with steroid abuse
    Steroid use by "power" field event athletes well
        documented
    Steroid use among sprinters not uncommon
    Swimmers among serious steroid offenders
    Use of steroids at Olympics not restricted to men

9. Russians among major early steroid users
    Soviet Communist Party ordered gov't officials to
        produce competitive athletes
    Experimentation by Soviet Olympic athletes well under
        way by mid-fifties
    Soviet Olympic athletes ordered to take straight
        testosterone for 1956 games
    Soviet weightlifters soon dominated the sport

10. East bloc countries big early users
    East German coaches now admit widespread use
    Virtually all East German sports affected
    East German athletes who refused to participate were
        dismissed from program
    East German experiments with "masking agents"

11. American involvement with steroids at games
    Dr. John Ziegler's 1956 visit with Russian trainer
    Ziegler begins prescribing steroids for weightlifter
        friends
    Ziegler's work with the CIBA Pharmaceutical Company
    Ziegler becomes disillusioned

12. Olympic steroid use into the 1980s
    '60's games a low point; no rules
    Many athletes admit to using to prepare for 1968
        games but none barred
    Moses claims nations were cutting deals by 1980
    Some suspect Soviet boycott of '84 games steroid-
        related

13. Steroid use at recent games
    Ben Johnson tests positive for steroid use at 1988 games
    Two Bulgarian weightlifters lose gold medals at 1988 games
    Steroid use still a problem at 1994 winter games

14. Estimates regarding steroid use by recent Olympians
    Edwin Moses estimates half of all top performers use
        steroids
    Lewis and Decker-Slaney claim majority use
    Dr. Clayton Thomas claims steroid use worse than ever
    David Steen claims use "rampant" in certain sports

15. IOC attempts to discourage steroid use
     Steroids added to list of banned substances in 1973
     Testing for steroids started at 1976 Montreal games
     Testing very sophisticated by 1984 games

16. Testing procedures
     Which athletes are tested
     How testing is actually conducted
     Technical aspects of testing

17. IOC penalties for using steroids

18. Why testing for steroids at Olympic Games has not been totally effective
     Athletes keep finding new "masking agents" to beat the tests
     Some athletes still beat tests by cycling use or using diuretics
     Random "out-of-competition" testing too expensive
     Many athletes getting by on technicalities
     Complex appeals process undercuts testing program
     Penalties have not always been consistent

19. Problems with the tests themselves
     Test results not always consistent or easy to read
     Mistakes have been made in testing
     The strange case of Ria van Landeghem at 1988 games

20. Hope for the future
     Ongoing steroid research continues to allow for better testing
     End of Cold War has increased potential for international cooperation

21. Reasons not to be too optimistic
     Coaches from major users in East bloc now all over the world
     New ways to hide steroid use constantly being found
     Motives for using anything to get a competitive edge more powerful than ever
     China seems to be picking up where Soviet bloc left off

22. Future scenarios?
     Public outrage could lead to total ban
     Blood testing could become economical and solve problem
     Use could become so common that public accepts

6.3.2. Convert the slug outline to a topic outline.

The second step in developing a detailed working outline involves converting the slug outline to a so-called "topic outline."

To create the slug outline you began by grouping together note cards with similar slugs. You then created super slugs to act as umbrellas for the cards that had been grouped together. In other words, you made slugs for the slugs.

Now you must carry that process a couple of steps further.

Taking into consideration both your preliminary question outline and your newly devised slug outline, you must now attempt to *group the groups*.

Take another look at the sample slug outline provided above. Notice how the first two groups deal in basic factual information about steroids themselves. They could probably be grouped together under a heading such as "Background information on steroids." Likewise, groups 3, 4, 5, and 6 all deal with forces that tempt Olympic athletes to use steroids, while groups 9 through 14 relate to the origin and progress of steroid use at the games. Accordingly, the former might be given a super heading such as "Why Olympic athletes use steroids," while "History of steroid abuse at the Olympic Games" might serve as an appropriate "super umbrella" for the latter.

Now take a close look at your own slug outline. Attempt to identify groups of note cards that have obvious relationships and create new super-super headings for these groups. With the major parts of your paper identified in your preliminary question outline always very much in mind, repeat the process until you have reached a level of subordination and organization with which you are comfortable and which will provide the framework (blueprint, road map) necessary for a well-organized paper.

When you have reached this point, assign traditional outlining numbers and letters according to the model provided below. Remember that it is not possible to divide anything into fewer than two parts and that you will need a Roman numeral II for every Roman numeral I, a capital letter B for every capital letter A, and so on:

I. (Roman numerals)
    A. (capital letters)
    B.
    (additional entries as needed)
        1. (Arabic numerals)
        2.
        (additional entries as needed)
            a. (lower case letters)
            b.
            (additional entries as needed)
                (1)(Arabic numerals in parentheses)
                (2)
                (additional entries as needed)
                    (a) (lower case letters in parentheses)
                    (b)(additional entries as needed)
II.
and so on . . .

    Note: This example shows five degrees of subordination. Not everyone will find it necessary to subordinate to this extent.

When you have finished assigning the traditional outlining numbers and letters, you will have completed your topic outline. It might look something like the example below:

Sample topic outline:

I. Background information on steroids
   A. Basic facts
      1. Origin and initial use of steroids
      2. What steroids are
      3. Definitions of <u>androgenic</u> and <u>anabolic</u>
   B. What steroids supposedly do for athletes
      1. Most experts believe steroids increase muscle mass and body weight
      2. Steroids are thought to increase strength and endurance
      3. Steroids may increase aggressiveness and hostility

II. Why some Olympic athletes are tempted to use steroids
   A. Some Olympians feel they need steroids just to compete
   B. Desire to win a strong motive for Olympic athletes to use steroids
      1. Desire to win almost obsessive among some athletes
      2. Dr. Goldman's research on desire to win
      3. Dr. Mirkin's question reveals overwhelming desire to win
   C. Greed an important factor in some Olympians' use of steroids
   D. Pressure from entire world of sports pushes athletes to do "whatever is necessary"
      1. Pressure comes from peers and teammates
      2. Coaches sometimes encourage athletes to use drugs
      3. Fans expect athletes to win at all costs

III. Olympic events most apt to involve the use of steroids
   A. Steroid use among Olympic weightlifters
      1. Olympic weightlifters generally thought to be first to use
      2. Olympic weightlifters believed to be among biggest abusers
      3. Problem so bad among weightlifters some think sport should be eliminated
   B. Other Olympic events involved with steroid abuse
      1. Steroid use by "power" field event athletes well documented
      2. Steroid use among sprinters not uncommon
      3. Swimmers among serious steroid offenders
      4. Use of steroids at Olympics not restricted to men

IV. History of steroid abuse at the Olympic Games
   A. Russians among major early steroid users
      1. Soviet Communist Party ordered gov't officials to produce competitive athletes
      2. Experimentation by Soviet Olympic athletes well under way by mid-fifties

      3. Soviet Olympic athletes ordered to take straight testosterone for 1956 games

      4. Soviet weightlifters soon dominated the sport

  B. East bloc countries big early users

      1. East German coaches now admit widespread use

      2. Virtually all East German sports affected

      3. East German athletes who refused to participate were dismissed from program

      4. East German experiments with "masking agents"

  C. American involvement with steroids at games

      1. Dr. John Ziegler's 1956 visit with Russian trainer

      2. Ziegler begins prescribing steroids for weightlifter friends

      3. Ziegler's work with the CIBA Pharmaceutical Company

      4. Ziegler becomes disillusioned

  D. Olympic steroid use into the 1980s

      1. Sixties games a low point; no rules

      2. Many athletes admit to using to prepare for 1968 games but none barred

      3. Moses claims nations were cutting deals by 1980

      4. Some suspect Soviet boycott of '84 games steroid-related

  E. Steroid use at recent games

      1. Athletes who tested positive at 1988 games

        a. Ben Johnson tests positive for steroid use at 1988 games

        b. Two Bulgarian weightlifters lose gold medals at 1988 games

      2. Estimates regarding steroid use by recent Olympians

        a. Edwin Moses estimates half of all top performers use steroids

        b. Lewis and Decker-Slaney claim majority use

        c. Dr. Clayton Thomas claims steroid use worse than ever

        d. David Steen claims use "rampant" in certain sports

      3. Steroid use still a problem at 1994 winter games

V.   Steps taken by the IOC to discourage steroid use

  A. History of testing

      1. Steroids added to list of banned substances in 1973

      2. Testing for steroids started at 1976 Montreal games

      3. Testing very sophisticated by 1984 games

  B. Testing procedures

      1. Which athletes are tested

      2. How testing is actually conducted

      3. Technical aspects of testing

  C. IOC penalties for using steroids

  D. Why testing has not been totally effective

      1. Problems with the tests themselves

        a. Test results not always consistent or easy to read

        b. Mistakes have been made in testing

        c. The strange case of Ria van Landeghem at 1988 games

      2. Athletes keep finding new "masking agents" to beat the tests

      3. Some athletes still beat tests by cycling use or using diuretics

      4. Random "out-of-competition" testing too expensive

            5. Many athletes getting by on technicalities
            6. Complex appeals process undercuts testing program
            7. Penalties have not always been consistent

    VI. What lies ahead?
         A. Hope for the future
            1. Ongoing steroid research continues to allow for
               better testing
            2. End of Cold War has increased potential for
               international cooperation
         B. Reasons not to be too optimistic
            1. IOC concentration on individual athlete a mistake
            2. Coaches from major users in East bloc now all over
               the world
            3. New ways to hide steroid use constantly being found
            4. Motives for using anything to get a competitive
               edge more powerful than ever
            5. China seems to be picking up where Soviet bloc left off
         C. Future scenarios?
            1. Public outrage could lead to total ban
            2. Blood testing could become economical and solve
               problem
            3. Use could become so common that public accepts

6.3.3. Re-evaluate the tentative thesis and revise it if necessary.

Remember the tentative thesis or hypothesis you developed in conjunction with your preliminary question outline? (Sections 3.4, 3.5, and 3.6) It was important to you at the time because it helped to give your research a sense of direction. It gave you a focal point—something to hang your hat on.

Now that you have immersed yourself in your subject, gathered the information necessary to write your paper, and organized that information in a way that makes sense, it is time to take one of the most important steps in the entire process of writing a research paper. It is time to take another look at that initial hypothesis.

Given what you have learned about your subject, does your tentative thesis still say *exactly* what you want it to say? Does it accurately and honestly reflect your thinking about your subject *now*? Can it still serve as a one-sentence summary for your entire paper, expressing as it should the very essence of your thinking, the very heart of your presentation? And finally, does it do all this without exaggeration? Remember that overstatement can be as damaging as misstatement or understatement. In short, make sure that you are not overreaching in your thesis statement—that you really do have the substance in your paper to back up the claim or claims that you will be posting there for all to see in your introduction.

If, after careful consideration, you believe that your tentative thesis meets these requirements, adopt it as the working thesis for your paper and place it at the top of the topic outline you have just developed, where it will remain highly visible as you compose the first draft of your paper.

If your tentative thesis does not meet these requirements, you will need to reshape it until you are absolutely certain that it says *exactly* what you want it to say, nothing more and nothing less.

Sample tentative (*initial*) thesis:

```
The use of anabolic steroids by Olympic athletes has been
occurring for a long time, but steps taken in recent years by the
International Olympic Committee have greatly reduced the problem.
```

Sample working (*revised*) thesis:

```
The use of anabolic steroids by Olympic athletes has been
occurring for a long time; but despite serious steps taken by
the International Olympic Committee to discourage such abuse,
the battle is far from over.
```

6.4. Something to keep in mind:

Once you have developed a detailed working outline and revised and updated your tentative thesis, you will be ready to begin composing the first draft of your paper. Remember, however, that even at this stage you may still find it necessary to change your plans. Strange things can happen in the writing process, and what looks neat and logical at this point may not actually turn out to be as neat and logical as it presently appears. Once again, that is why the end product of the process described above is called a *working* outline. It is still subject to change and may well require additional adjusting before your paper is complete.

This is not something to be concerned about. Just remember that nothing is ever final until it is final—in this case, until it is turned in to your instructor and is no longer in your hands.

Step 7
Writing the Rough Draft

7.1. What is a rough draft?

Now that you have collected the brick and mortar for your paper in your note cards and established a blueprint or plan for its construction in your detailed working outline, you are ready to make your first attempt at actually "building" the paper. This initial or preliminary effort to move beyond the note cards and the outline, to begin to put thoughts and ideas together in written form, whether on a computer screen or on paper, is called writing the rough draft. This writing is *rough* in the sense that it lacks the polish and refinement of later drafts or of a final copy. That it is called a *draft*, sometimes a *first draft*, implies that revision is expected and that later attempts will follow.

7.2. Why should I bother with a rough draft?

Good question. Why not do it right the first time and be finished with it?

The answer is simple. Putting together a quality research paper, even after having successfully completed the note-taking and outlining processes, requires careful work in a variety of areas—adequate development of and support for the main ideas, a clear and logical organizational scheme, graceful transition between paragraphs and major parts, appropriate documentation, a pleasing style, correct spelling, and acceptable punctuation, to name only a few.

Unfortunately, few people have the ability or the inclination to concentrate on more than a few of these components at a time, and most have their hands full just focusing on one or two of them.

Doing a rough draft, composing from the outset with the understanding that modification and refinement will be possible at a later time, gives the writer the sense of freedom needed to jump in and get the project under way without worrying too much about getting everything exactly right the first time through. It makes it possible to concentrate on the essential task of constructing the basic building without being sidetracked at every turn by concern about the choice of floor covering or wallpaper.

7.3. How do I go about writing a rough draft?

7.3.1. Assemble the necessary material.

The two most important items you will need to complete this task successfully are your detailed working outline, complete with thesis statement, and your note cards, sorted into piles corresponding to the various headings in your detailed working outline.

If you have access to a computer equipped with word processing software, by all means take advantage of it. (Word processors significantly improve most people's ability to compose, and they make revision easy.) If you do not, make sure that you have a generous supply of lined paper and a good pen or pencil.

7.3.2. Work your plan.

Following your outline carefully, reviewing your note cards periodically, and always keeping one eye on your thesis statement, begin developing your paper a section at a time. Concentrate on getting down your major thoughts and ideas, not on correctness or refinement. There will be ample opportunity later to fix up and smooth out the rough spots.

7.3.3. Support generalizations with particulars.

Bear in mind that, as is true of any written composition, your research paper will be as interesting and convincing as it is *specific*. Do your best to back up your points and arguments with facts, illustrations, and examples, most of which should be found in the notes you have so carefully collected.

7.3.4. Leave room for later changes.

This need not be a consideration if you are working on a word processor, but if you must compose your rough draft the old-fashioned way, with paper and pencil, be sure to leave yourself plenty of room for revisions and corrections. Write only on every other or even every third line, and leave yourself wide margins on either side. *Never* use the back side of a page. (Trying to save a few cents on paper at this stage of the game is a foolish economy indeed!)

7.4. What is documentation, and when is it necessary?

As you develop your rough draft, you will no doubt have occasion to incorporate into it—whether restated in your own words as a paraphrase or a summary, or quoted directly—information, facts, statistics, thoughts, and opinions that are not original with you, that you have read about or learned from others.

To be fair to those from whom you got your material and to make it possible for your readers to check your research or simply to satisfy their own curiosity about your subject, you must *document* information and ideas thus gleaned from others. To document means to provide the reader with information regarding the origin or source of any material that did not originate with you. (More about the *how* later.)

All direct quotations must be documented. In other words, sources must be acknowledged and credit must be given.

Paraphrased and summarized material—material that you have re-formed into your own words—must also frequently be documented.

The catch has to do with whether such material can fairly be considered common knowledge, not in the sense that every man or woman on the street would know about it, but in the sense that anyone familiar with your subject would know about it.

The best way to know whether information you are using is or is not common knowledge is to ask yourself how often you came across it in your research. If the information you are using, even if you are putting it into you own words, is information that you were able to locate in *one source and only one source*, it is probably not common knowledge and should therefore be documented. (Note that most analyses, arguments, ideas, thoughts, and opinions will fall into this category and will need to be documented.) If, on the other hand, the information seemed widely available, and especially if it was not documented within the sources in which you found it, it probably fits the definition of common knowledge, and you may thus be comfortable not documenting it.

A word of caution is in order, however. It is better to be too cautious about citing material you are using than not cautious enough. *When in doubt, document!*

7.5. How should I deal with documentation in my rough draft?

The simplest way to document material in your rough draft, and indeed, the preferred MLA (Modern Language Association) method for documenting material, even in the final draft of your paper, is to provide information about your sources right in the text of the paper itself, typically in parentheses immediately following the material being documented. Such documentation is known as parenthetical or in-line documentation and is much simpler to use than the more traditional method of documenting in the form of footnotes (notes appearing at the *foot* of the page) or endnotes (notes appearing at the *end* of the paper).

Parenthetical documentation generally requires two pieces of information: (1) a link to the bibliography card for the source from which the information was taken, usually an author's last name, and (2) precise information regarding just where in the source the material can be found, in most cases a page number, but occasionally volume numbers, acts, scenes, and the like.

As you write your rough draft, document material you are borrowing parenthetically, taking your cue from the examples given below. (Keep in mind that information about the source already provided in the text of your paper, an author's last name, for example, may be omitted from the documentation.)

7.5.1. For a work written by a single author (author's name already given in text):

Since the bibliographic link (the author's last name) has already been provided, the only documentation necessary is a page number. Note that unless the material being documented is a direct quotation being set off from the rest of the text, the documentation occurs within the closing punctuation.

```
As Jonathan Harris notes, because steroids allow the body
to store increased amounts of nitrogen, thus enhancing the
development of protein, they can also contribute to
substantial increases in strength and endurance (88).
```

7.5.2. For a work written by a single author (author's name not provided in text):

Give the last name of the author or agency responsible for the work and the page number or numbers on which the material or information appeared. Leave a space between the author's last name and the page number but do not separate the two items with any mark of punctuation.

```
Because steroids allow the body to store increased amounts
of nitrogen, thus enhancing the development of protein,
they can also contribute to substantial increases in
strength and endurance (Harris 88).
```

7.5.3. For a work written by more than one author:

Cite the last name of each author given in the order in which they appear on your bibliography card, which may or may not be alphabetical. For a work written by two authors, simply join the two last names with the word and. Follow the name of the second author with the page number or numbers. (See the example below.) For a work written by three authors, insert commas between the last names of the authors listed and an and between the names of the second and third authors listed. (e.g., Goldman, Bush, and Klatz 73) For a work written by four or more authors, follow the last name of the first author listed with the Latin phrase et al., meaning "and others." (e.g. Johnson, et al. 68)

```
If the first urine specimen taken immediately following
competition tests positive, a second sample is taken in
the presence of a committee member from the athlete's
national organization (O'Brien and Cohen 242).
```

7.5.4. For a work without known authorship:

If the authorship for a work is unknown, draw the link to your bibliography card with the next available piece of information on the card, usually a title. If the title is more than a few words, give only the first two or three. (For example, "Olympic Roundup: Austrian Bobsledder Flunks Steroid Test" may be shortened to "Olympic Roundup.")

```
At the 1994 Winter Olympic Games in Lillehammer, Norway, a
veteran Austrian bobsled driver named Gerhard Rainer was
sent home and banned from further competition for a two-
year period after testing positive for steroids ("Olympic
Roundup" C5).
```

7.5.5. For a work by an author for whom you have more than one bibliography card:

Since providing only a last name would still leave a reader guessing as to exactly which source was being cited, you will need to provide a title in addition to the author's last name. (Once again, if the title is only a word or two, as is the case below, it should be given in full. If it is more than a word or two, it should be shortened to the first two or three words.)

```
Early Soviet Olympic athletes suffered greatly for their
experimentation with performance-enhancing drugs (Nuwer,
Steroids 27).
```

7.6. A few words about direct quotations:

Avoid the temptation to let your paper become a mere collage of direct quotations, strung together with the glue of linking phrases and transitional sentences. Remember the advice given in Step 4 on note-taking. Quote directly only when the material you are citing is *more concise, more convincing,* or *more colorful* than your paraphrase could be.

If you do find it advisable to use a direct quotation, do your best to work it into your paper as smoothly as possible. One way to do this is to integrate the quotation into one of your own sentences, as is illustrated in the example below:

```
At least one expert on the subject believes that "the
Soviet bloc nations boycotted the 1984 Olympic Games . . .
because they feared a sophisticated drug-testing system
might expose their use of steroids and other illegal
substances" (Nuwer 36).
```

Another way is to lead up to the quoted material with an appropriate introductory sentence. (Note that in such situations the introductory sentence is often followed by a colon.)

```
In "The Molecules of Sport," Rosellini, Lynn, and Schrof
note with dismay the situation following the demise of one
of the more aggressive steroid abuse programs in the
former East bloc:
          To date, virtually no one has been punished for
          the East German doping experiments—except the
          athletes who suffered harmful effects. In fact,
          since many of the leading researchers have now
          fled the former East bloc, steroid technology will
          likely proliferate. Science rarely goes backward—
          even if those controlling it sometimes do (57).
```

Unless you wish to draw special attention to it, a quotation of four or fewer lines is usually run into the text, as in the first example above. Direct quotations of more than four lines are typically set off or indented from the left margin 10 spaces if you are using a typewriter or approximately three quarters of an inch if you are doing your work on a computer. In such cases the indentation takes the place of quotation marks.

7.7. Something to think about:

Most students regard writing the rough draft as the most difficult step in the entire research paper process. Such feelings are understandable. This is, after all, where you do finally have to come to grips with your research findings and organize those findings in a way that provides convincing support for your thesis. In short, this is where it all must come together.

Whatever else you do as you begin this admittedly crucial step, however, keep in mind that you are writing a *rough draft*, not a final copy. Nobody expects it to be perfect, and neither should you.

So if things do not work out precisely as planned or if you are not sure you are getting things down exactly the way you should, do not be overly concerned. Remember, this is your opportunity to take some chances, to spread your wings a bit, to experiment, to make mistakes. You will have ample time later to fix things up, to put on those finishing touches, to make it a masterpiece.

Step 8
Revising the Rough Draft

8.1. What does it mean to revise the rough draft?

To revise a rough draft means to rework it until you are fully satisfied that it says *exactly* what you want it to say (no more and no less), and that it says it in the very best way possible.

In your rough draft you painted with a broad brush; you sculpted with a crude chisel. You got your basic thoughts and ideas down; but things probably are, well, a bit unpolished. Now it is time to go back over this diamond in the rough and find the jewel in it, to work with finer tools, to give all those little details the attention they deserve.

8.2. Why is revising the rough draft so important?

Very few people get things exactly right the first time out. Indeed, the old myth about authors or composers waking up in the middle of the night to scrawl down entire poems or symphonic movements in fits of inspiration, never to change a word or a note, is for the most part exactly that—myth. Great art does not typically happen that way, and neither do good research papers.

Instead, the vast majority of quality research papers are, like their counterparts in the world of literature, music, painting, and sculpture, the result of rigorous and meticulous crafting and re-crafting. Words and phrases are changed and changed again. Entire paragraphs are rearranged, rewritten, even thrown out altogether in favor of new attempts. In short, everything in the paper gets close scrutiny—the content, the organization, the style, even the basics like spelling and punctuation.

For most writers the result of such careful reworking is a much improved product, to say nothing of a vastly increased sense of pride and accomplishment.

8.3. How do I go about revising my rough draft?

8.3.1. Begin by checking for content.

Take another look at your thesis. Then read over your rough draft carefully to make sure that you have actually *supported* that thesis.

Specifically, you need to be asking yourself two questions: (1) Have I included everything I should have included to support my thesis *fully* and *completely*, or are there gaps in my material? Have I left things out that really need to be in this paper? and (2) Is the material that I have included the material that I should have included? In other words, is it all *directly* related to the support or development of my thesis, or have I drifted from my subject now and then? (Remember that the concept of unity, of sticking to the topic, is an important concept in all good writing, including the research paper.)

8.3.2. Check for appropriate organization and transition.

Again, you must ask yourself two questions: (1) Does the arrangement of the subparts and individual paragraphs of the paper follow a clear and logical plan? and (2) Is the relationship of each subpart and individual paragraph to the immediately preceding subpart or individual paragraph (and to the thesis itself) sufficiently clear?

One of the best ways to make sure that your paper hangs together the way it should is to read through it rapidly, *aloud*. If you can get a family member or a friend to sit down with you as you do this, so much the better. In fact, it might even be a good idea to have someone else read your paper aloud to you so that you can concentrate all of your attention on things like quality of organization.

8.3.3. Check the research material.

First, this means double checking every quotation against the note from which it was taken to make sure that you have transferred the material accurately. It also means taking another look at all quotations and paraphrases to make sure that you have used them appropriately and honestly, that you are playing fair with your sources by honoring original context and intention, at least insofar as you can know it.

Checking your research material also means making certain that everything that should be documented is documented. (Perhaps this would be a good time to return to Step 5 to reread the section on plagiarism. Remember that using other people's material in your paper without giving proper credit is a serious offense.) Be sure to document *all* direct quotations, *all* original opinions or interpretations, and *any* statistical or factual information not found in a variety of sources.

Finally, be sure that you have provided smooth transition into and away from quotations (refer to the section on quotations in Step 7) and that you have included all necessary punctuation around the quotations you have used— quotation marks, ellipsis marks, brackets. (See examples in Step 5.)

8.3.4. Examine the style in which your paper has been written.

■ Avoid using the first or second person (*I* or *you*). Your paper should not be stiff or unnecessarily formal, but neither should it be chatty or overly casual.

- Avoid using the passive voice unless you have some special reason for doing so. For example, prefer "the author noted" to "it was noted by the author."
- Avoid slang and breezy informalities.
- Avoid unnecessary wordiness. Do not use 20 words to say what you can say in 10; and never, never pad your paper just to meet a specified length requirement. Teachers can see right through such practices and are not impressed.
- Develop compound and complex sentences through the use of subordination and combination.
- Vary sentence beginnings and length.

Note: One of the very best resources on style continues to be *The Elements of Style* by William Strunk, Jr. and E.B. White. This little book, barely 70 pages in length and now over 30 years old, is as timely today as it ever was. Ask your instructor or your library media specialist for a copy.

8.3.5. Check for correct spelling, punctuation, and usage.

- If you have used a word processor to compose your rough draft, be sure to run the spell checker. If the program you are using has a grammar and style checker, run that too. If you have had to do without a computer and you are in doubt about a word's correct spelling, look it up in a good dictionary. Neither laziness nor carelessness is excusable in a project like this.
- Check to see that all sentences are complete, reasonably smooth, and appropriately punctuated. Reading through your paper aloud should go a long way toward helping you check for the former. If in doubt about the latter, consult a reputable punctuation handbook.
- Check for proper pronoun/antecedent and subject/verb agreement.
- Be consistent in your use of tense and person.

8.4. If your instructor requires it, change your parenthetical documentation to a more traditional format.

When you composed your rough draft, you documented your sources parenthetically, right in the text of your paper. This is the method preferred by the Modern Language Association and an increasing number of teachers. If your instructor accepts such documentation, you may ignore this section.

If your instructor expects the more traditional *footnotes* (documentation in the form of a note at the *foot* of the page) or *endnotes* (documentation appearing altogether at the *end* of your paper), however, it is now time to replace your parenthetical documentation with slightly raised, consecutively numbered, Arabic numerals (beginning with 1) and to compose full-fledged notes (with corresponding numerals) supplying more detailed information about your sources in a format consistent with the examples given below. (See Appendices D, E, and F to see how such documentation should appear in an actual paper.)

If you are using a word processor, making this conversion should be easy. Most word processing programs have provisions for handling both footnotes and endnotes, even for inserting superscript, the slightly raised numerals that you will need to use to link the material you are citing to the note describing the source from which it came. (Check the manual that came with your software if you are uncertain about the procedure.)

If you are revising your rough draft by hand (planning to type your final copy or to write out your final copy by hand), replace your parenthetical documentation with consecutively numbered Arabic numerals. Compose the notes themselves (with corresponding numerals) on a *separate* sheet of paper. Do this regardless of whether you plan to do footnotes or endnotes in your final copy.

In any case, if your note is a first-time reference to a source (a *primary* citation), choose from among the forms shown below:

8.5. Sample footnotes and endnotes

8.5.1. Nonreference books (first citation only)

a. A book written by a single author:

[1] Edward F. Dolan, <u>Drugs in Sports</u>, rev. ed. (New York: Franklin Watts, 1992) 21.

b. A book written by two or three authors:

[2] Gary E. McCuen and Ronald P. Swanson, <u>Toxic Nightmare: Ecocide in the USSR & Eastern Europe</u> (Hudson, WI: Gary E. McCuen, 1993) 37.

[2] Martin Collcutt, Marius Jansen, and Isao Kumakura, <u>Cultural Atlas of Japan</u> (New York: Facts on File, 1988) 104.

c. A book written by more than three authors:

[3] Neil Barron, et al., <u>1990 What Do I Read Next? A Reader's Guide to Current Genre Fiction</u> (Detroit: Gale, 1991) 79.

d. A book authored by a corporation, commission, association, or committee:

[4] The World Bank, <u>World Development Report 1993</u> (New York: Oxford UP, 1993) 56.

e. A book authored by a government body or agency:

> [5] Washington State, Office of Financial Management, Forecasting Division, <u>Washington State 1993 Data Book</u> (Olympia: Washington State Department of Printing, 1993) 49.

> [5] United States Department of Commerce, Economics and Statistics Administration, Bureau of the Census, <u>Statistical Abstract of the United States 1992</u>, 122nd ed. (Washington: GPO, 1992) 234.

f. A book with an editor or compiler instead of an author:

> [6] Phyllis M. Martin and Patrick O'Meara, eds., <u>Africa</u>, 2nd ed. (Bloomington: Indiana UP, 1986) 267.

g. A book that has been republished (such as a classic novel re-issued in paperback):

> [7] Mark Twain, <u>The Adventures of Huckleberry Finn</u> (1884; Topeka: Econo-Clad, 1985) 176.

h. A selection from an anthology or collection:

> [8] Edgar Allan Poe, "The Tell-Tale Heart," <u>The Oxford Book of American Short Stories</u>, ed. Joyce Carol Oates (New York: Oxford UP, 1992) 91-96.

8.5.2. Reference books (first citation only)

a. An article or entry from a general encyclopedia (such as *World Book*, *Americana*, or *Britannica*):

> [9] Odie B. Faulk, "Western Frontier Life," <u>The World Book Encyclopedia</u>, 1993 ed.

b. An article or entry from a *single-volume* reference work:

> [10] John Steele Gordon, "Iron and Steel Industry," <u>The Reader's Companion to American History</u>, eds. Eric Foner and John A. Garraty (Boston: Houghton Mifflin, 1991) 574.

c. An article or entry from a *multivolume* reference work (volumes *not* individually titled):

> [11] Frederick D. Weil, "Political Party Systems," <u>Encyclopedia of Sociology</u>, gen. eds. Edgar F. Borgatta and Marie L. Borgatta, vol. 3 (New York: Macmillan, 1992) 1486.

d. An article or entry from a *multivolume* reference work (each volume individually titled):

> [12] Susan Buck Sutton, "Greeks," <u>Encyclopedia of World Cultures: Europe</u>, ed. Linda A. Bennett, vol. 4 of <u>Encyclopedia of World Cultures</u> (Boston: G. K. Hall, 1992) 133, 1981-1995.

8.5.3. Periodical material (first citation only)

a. An article or story from a newspaper:

> [13] Dana Millbank, "Little Luxemberg Sees a Big Problem," <u>The Wall Street Journal</u> 31 March 1994, western ed.: A11.

b. An article or story from a magazine:

> [14] Michael D. Lemonick, "Too Many Fish in the Sea," <u>Time</u> 4 April 1994: 63.

c. An article or story from a scholarly journal:

> [15] Ted Galen Carpenter, "Closing the Nuclear Umbrella," <u>Foreign Affairs</u> 73.2 (1994): 63.

8.5.4. Reprinted material (first citation only)

a. Previously published articles in collections and anthologies (such as *Social Issues Resources Series* or *Opposing Viewpoints*):

> [16] Jere Longman, "From Soweto, It's a Hard Run to Glory," <u>Philadelphia Inquirer</u> 14 June 1992: A1, rpt. in <u>Sports</u>, vol. 4 (Boca Raton: Social Issues Resources Series, 1993) art. 34.

> [16] Leonard Weiss, "Tighten Up on Nuclear Cheaters," <u>Bulletin of the Atomic Scientists</u> May 1991, rpt. as "The International Atomic Energy Agency is Ineffective," <u>Nuclear Proliferation: Opposing Viewpoints</u> (San Diego: Greenhaven, 1992) 74.

8.5.5. Nonprint material (first citation only)

a. A lecture, speech, or address:

> [17] David Barber, "The United States and Pacific Rim Trade," Fort Vancouver High School Contemporary World Problems Class, Vancouver, WA, 28 March 1994.

b. A television or radio program:

> [18] "What is Money Anyway?" narr. Christopher Castile, prod. and writ. Jane Paley and Larry Price, <u>Step by Step, Money Made Easy: The ABC Kids' Guide to Dollars and Sense</u>, ABC Saturday Special, KATU, Portland, OR, 2 April 1994.

c. A personal interview:

> [19] Donald L. Peterson, personal interview, 1 April 1994.

8.5.6. Computer-accessed material (first citation only)

a. Computer software:

> [20] <u>PC Globe</u>, vers. 4.0, computer software, PC Globe, 1990, MS DOS 2.0+, 512KB, disk.

b. CD-ROM software:

> [21] John K. B. Ford, "Whale," <u>Information Finder</u>, vers. 2.4, computer software, World Book, 1993, MS-DOS 3.1+, CD-ROM.

c. Material from online information services (such as *BRS* or *Dialog*):

> [22] Sharon Robb Reuters, "U.S. Coaches Credit China's Rapid Rise to 'Pharmaceutical Warfare,'" <u>Seattle Times</u> 5 December 1993, weekend ed.: C12 (Dialog file 707, item 07339158).

d. Material from online news services (such as *X-Press*):

> [23] "Clinton Pushes Health Plan," Associated Press, Troy, NC, 5 April 1994, X-Press Information Services, 15:35:33.

8.5.7. Forms to be used for second-time or *secondary* citations:

Once a source has been cited in full, subsequent references to the same source may be shortened considerably. Generally speaking, it is sufficient to provide the author's last name and the appropriate page number or numbers. For example:

> [24] Harris 87.

If an author's name is not available, use the first item in the bibliographic citation, whatever that might be—usually a title. For example:

> [24] "Johnson Used Steroids" 46.

If your bibliography contains more than one source by the same author, you will need to provide both the author's last name and at least a shortened version of the title. For example:

24 Nuwer, <u>Steroids</u> 25.

Note: The Modern Language Association no longer recommends the use of *Ibid.* and *Op. cit.* in secondary citations.

8.5.8. Things to keep in mind about documenting your sources in footnotes or endnotes:

■ The first line of a note should be indented about three eighths of an inch (five spaces if you are using a typewriter); the second line (if there is one) should come back to the margin.

■ The number placed before the note should be slightly raised and unadorned with punctuation of any kind. One space should separate it from the note itself.

■ Notes are numbered consecutively throughout the paper, beginning with 1. (Every note gets its own number.)

■ Information provided to the reader in the text of the paper (author's name, title) need not be repeated in the note.

■ The following abbreviations may be used in notes when certain information is not available:

n.d.	no date (no space between)
n.p.	no place of publication; no publisher (no space between)
n. pag.	no pagination (space between)

■ Footnotes should be single-spaced, but you should double-space between them. Endnotes should be double-spaced, and you should double-space between them.

8.6. Compile your final bibliography

You must include with your final paper either a complete list of all the sources that you found useful in writing your paper (even if you did not make direct reference to them in your writing), or at the very least, a complete list of the sources that you have actually cited in your paper. In compiling this list, choose from among the forms that follow:

8.7. Sample bibliographic citations

8.7.1. Nonreference books

a. A book written by a single author:

> Dolan, Edward F. <u>Drugs in Sports</u>. Rev. ed. New
> York: Franklin Watts, 1992.

b. A book written by two or three authors:

> McCuen, Gary E., and Ronald P. Swanson. <u>Toxic
> Nightmare: Ecocide in the USSR & Eastern Europe.</u>
> Hudson, WI: Gary E. McCuen, 1993.

> Collcutt, Martin, Marius Jansen, and Isao Kumakura.
> <u>Cultural Atlas of Japan</u>. New York: Facts on
> File, 1988.

c. A book written by more than three authors:

> Barron, Neil, et al. <u>1990 What Do I Read Next? A
> Reader's Guide to Current Genre Fiction</u>.
> Detroit: Gale, 1991.

d. A book authored by a corporation, commission, association, or committee:

> The World Bank. <u>World Development Report 1993</u>. New York:
> Oxford UP, 1993.

e. A book authored by a government body or agency:

> Washington State. Office of Financial Management.
> Forecasting Division. <u>Washington State 1993
> Data Book</u>. Olympia: Washington State Department
> of Printing, 1993.

> United States Department of Commerce. Economics and
> Statistics Administration. Bureau of the
> Census. <u>Statistical Abstract of the United
> States 1992</u>. 122nd ed. Washington: GPO, 1992.

f. A book with an editor or compiler instead of an author:

> Martin, Phyllis M., and Patrick O'Meara, eds. <u>Africa</u>.
> 2nd ed. Bloomington: Indiana UP, 1986.

g. A book that has been republished (such as a classic novel re-issued in paperback):

```
Twain, Mark.  The Adventures of Huckleberry Finn.
     1884.  Topeka: Econo-Clad, 1985.
```

h. A selection from an anthology or collection:

```
Poe, Edgar Allan.  "The Tell-Tale Heart."  The Oxford
     Book of American Short Stories.  Ed. Joyce Carol
     Oates.  New York: Oxford UP, 1992.  91-96.
```

8.7.2. Reference books

a. An article or entry from a general encyclopedia (such as *World Book*, *Americana*, or *Britannica*):

```
Faulk, Odie B.  "Western Frontier Life."  The World
     Book Encyclopedia.  1993 ed.
```

b. An article or entry from a *single-volume* reference work:

```
Gordon, John Steele.  "Iron and Steel Industry."  The
     Reader's Companion to American History.  Eds.
     Eric Foner and John A. Garraty.  Boston:
     Houghton Mifflin, 1991.  574-575.
```

c. An article or entry from a *multivolume* reference work (volumes *not* individually titled):

```
Weil, Frederick D.  "Political Party Systems."
     Encyclopedia of Sociology.  Gen. eds. Edgar F.
     Borgatta and Marie L. Borgatta.  Vol. 3.  New
     York: Macmillan, 1992.  1485-92.  4 vols.
```

d. An article or entry from a *multivolume* reference work (each volume *individually* titled):

```
Sutton, Susan Buck.  "Greeks."  Encyclopedia of World
     Cultures: Europe.  Ed. Linda A. Bennett.  Vol.
     4 of Encyclopedia of World Cultures.  Boston:
     G. K. Hall, 1992.  131-34.  10 vols.  Gen. ed.
     David Levinson.  1991-1995.
```

8.7.3. Periodical material

a. An article or story from a newspaper:

```
Millbank, Dana.  "Little Luxemberg Sees a Big Problem."  The
     Wall Street Journal 31 March 1994, Western ed.: A11.
```

b. An article or story from a magazine:

```
Lemonick, Michael D.  "Too Few Fish in the Sea."
        Time 4 April 1994: 70-71.
```

c. An article or story from a scholarly journal:

```
Carpenter, Ted Galen.  "Closing the Nuclear Umbrella."
        Foreign Affairs 73.2 (1994): 9-13.
```

8.7.4. Reprinted material

a. Previously published articles in collections and anthologies (such as *Social Issues Resources Series* and *Opposing Viewpoints*):

```
Longman, Jere.  "From Soweto, It's a Hard Run to
        Glory."  Philadelphia Inquirer (14 June 1992):
        A1+.  Rpt. in Sports, Vol. 1.  Boca Raton:
        Social Issues Resources Series, 1993.  Art. 34.
```

```
Weiss, Leonard.  "Tighten Up on Nuclear Cheaters."
        Bulletin of the Atomic Scientists (May 1991):
        Rpt. as "The International Atomic Energy Agency
        Is Ineffective."  Nuclear Proliferation:
        Opposing Viewpoints.  San Diego: Greenhaven,
        1992.  73-78.
```

8.7.5. Nonprint material

a. A lecture, speech, or address:

```
Barber, David.  "The United States and Pacific Rim Trade."
        Fort Vancouver High School Contemporary World
        Problems Class.  Vancouver, WA, 24 March 1994.
```

b. A television or radio program:

```
"What is Money Anyway?"  Narr. Christopher Castile.
        Prod. and Writ. Jane Paley and Larry Price.
        Step by Step, Money Made Easy: The ABC Kids'
        Guide to Dollars and Sense.  ABC Saturday
        Special.  KATU, Portland, OR.  2 April 1994.
```

c. A personal interview:

```
Peterson, Donald.  Personal interview.  1 April 1994.
```

8.7.6. Computer-accessed material

a. Computer software:

```
PC Globe.  Vers. 4.0.  Computer software.  PC Globe,
     1990.  MS DOS 2.0+, 512KB, disk.
```

b. CD-ROM software:

```
Ford, John K. B.  "Whale."  Information Finder.  Vers.
     2.4.  Computer software.  World Book, 1993.  MS-
     DOS 3.1+, CD-ROM.
```

c. Material from online information services (such as *BRS* or *Dialog*):

```
Reuters, Sharon Robb.  "U.S. Coaches Credit China's
     Rapid Rise to 'Pharmaceutical Warfare.'"
     Seattle Times 5 December 1993: C12.  Dialog file
     707, item 07339158.
```

d. Material from online news services (such as *X-Press*):

```
"Clinton Pitches Health Plan."  Associated Press.
     Troy, NC, 5 April 1994.  X-Press Information
     Services, 15:35:33.
```

8.7.7. Things to keep in mind about bibliographic entries:

- The first line of a bibliographic entry begins on the margin. The second line, if there is one, is indented approximately three eighths of an inch (five spaces if you are using a typewriter). *Note that this is just the opposite of the form used for notes.*
- Bibliographic entries are *not* numbered. Instead, they are listed *alphabetically,* according to the authors' last names or according to the first word of the title (excluding *a, an,* and *the*) if an author's name has not been given.
- The same abbreviations used in notes when certain information is not available may be used in bibliographic entries.
- When a bibliography includes more than one title by the same author, the selections are listed alphabetically according to the first word of the title (again excluding *a, an,* and *the*). In such cases the author's name is given with the first entry only. For the second and subsequent entries three unspaced hyphens followed by a period are substituted for the author's name. For example:

```
Nuwer, Hank.  Sports Scandals.  Chicago: Franklin Watts, 1994.

---. Steroids. New York: Franklin Watts, 1990.
```

- Bibliographic entries should be double-spaced.

Step 9
Preparing and Assembling the Final Copy

9.1. What is *format*, and what do I need to know about it?

The term format refers to the physical appearance of your paper—literally, the *form* it takes on the page. As such, it has to do with things like type, margins, spacing, and pagination.

Absolute consensus or agreement regarding acceptable format for the final copy of a research paper does not exist. For this reason it may be a good idea to check with your instructor to see if he or she has strong preferences in this area.

The suggestions made below conform to standards widely used and will probably be acceptable to most teachers:

9.1.1. Type

If at all possible, type your final copy or use a word processor and print your final copy on a letter quality or laser printer. Handwritten final copies may be approved in rare instances but are becoming less and less acceptable. Use a black ribbon for typing or printing. If you must handwrite your paper, stick to black or blue ink.

9.1.2. Paper

Whether you type, print, or handwrite your final copy, use good quality, standard-sized, 8½ x 11 inch white paper. (Avoid onion skin or easy-erase paper.)

9.1.3. Margins

Allow a one-inch margin both left and right, as well as at top and bottom. Use one side of the page only.

9.1.4. Indentation

Paragraphs, footnotes, and endnotes should be indented three eighths of an inch if you are using a word processor, five spaces if you are using a typewriter. Direct quotations of more than four lines are set off from the left margin approximately three quarters of an inch if you are using a word processor and 10 spaces if you are using a typewriter.

9.1.5. Spacing

Double-space your entire paper, with the exception of footnotes, which should be single-spaced. (You should double-space between footnotes, however.)

9.1.6. Pagination

All page numbers should be placed in the upper right-hand corner of the page, on the margin and approximately one half inch from the top. It is a good idea for students to place their last name immediately in front of each page number. (See appendixes for examples.)

9.1.7. Corrections

If you are using a word processor, make *all* corrections on the computer before making a printed copy. If you are using a typewriter or if you are handwriting your paper and your mistakes cannot be fixed up with correcting tape or fluid, draw a single horizontal line through the text that needs to be changed and make your revisions as neatly as possible *above* the line. If you need to do this more than once or twice on a page, re-do the page.

9.1.8. Bindings

When you have finished compiling the final copy of your paper, staple it once in the upper left-hand corner or fasten it with a single paper clip. Avoid fancy covers and binders.

9.2. What are the parts I need to include in the final copy of my paper? In what order should they appear? What, if any, are their unique formatting requirements?

Precisely what parts will go into making up the whole of your research paper will depend both on your instructor's requirements and on your own particular preferences as a writer. Obviously, all papers will need to include a *body*, and nearly all instructors will want to see a bibliography or list of works cited; but beyond that the picture is less clear. Check with your teacher regarding his or her requirements.

Regardless of your instructor's requirements, the *order* in which the following parts are listed and the *formatting* instructions given below are widely accepted.

9.2.1. A title page (Check with your instructor.)

If your paper does *not* contain any so-called "front matter" such as a preface or an outline and if your instructor approves, you may be able to dispense with a separate title page by providing the information traditionally included on the title page at the top of the first page of the text of the paper. This is actually the Modern Language Association's preference. (See Appendix C for an example.)

If your paper *does* include front matter of any kind, however, and in any case if your instructor prefers that you include a separate title page, provide the following information in the format specified below: (See Appendix A for an example.)

- The *title* of the paper, centered, approximately a third of the way down from the top of the page. (Capitalize the first letter of all significant words in the title.)
- Your *name*, centered, approximately a third of the way from the bottom of the page.
- Your *instructor's name*, centered, immediately below your own name.
- The *name of the class* for which you are submitting the paper, centered, immediately below the name of your instructor.
- The *date*, centered, immediately below the name of the class.

Do *not* number the title page, even though it is really page *i* of your paper.

9.2.2. A preface (Optional)

A preface may be included to explain something unique about your paper (how you gathered your information, for example, or how you have chosen to present it) or to give credit to people other than your instructor who have been especially helpful to you as you wrote your paper.

If you include a preface, adhere to the format specified below:

- Give your preface the simple heading of Preface, centered and positioned approximately one inch from the top of the page.
- Because a preface is considered front matter, as is the title page, the page number should be given in lower case Roman numerals. (Since the title page, should your paper contain one, is actually page *i*, your preface, should you decide to include one, will be page *ii*.

9.2.3. An outline (Check with your instructor.)

Your instructor may ask you to include with your paper an outline, complete with an appropriately designated thesis sentence or statement.

If you are asked to include the plan for your paper, adhere to the following guidelines: (See Appendix B for an example.)

Give your outline the simple heading of Outline, centered and positioned approximately one inch from the top of the page.

In setting up your outline, be sure to adhere to the accepted numbering and lettering system. (If in doubt, refer to the treatment of this subject given in Step 6.)

Like title pages and prefaces, outlines are considered front matter. Accordingly, page numbers for outlines should be given in lower-case Roman numerals.

9.2.4. The body (No choice about this one)

Keep in mind the following in putting together the text of your paper: (See Appendices C, D, and E for examples.)

A slightly larger margin may be provided at the top of the opening page— up to one and a half inches.

The pages of the body should be numbered with standard Arabic numerals, beginning with 1. On the opening page this number may be omitted, although the page remains in fact page number 1. The second page is, of course, page number 2.

Remember to allow for extra indentation for direct quotations that you have decided to set off, either because of their length or because you wish to draw special attention to them. Standard practice is to give such set-off material double the left margin indentation that you provide for the opening of a paragraph. (See 9.1.4, "Indentation")

9.2.5. An appendix or appendixes (Optional)

An appendix or a series of appendixes may be used to include graphs, tables, or illustrative material too cumbersome to be incorporated into the text of your paper.

If you chose to include an appendix (or appendixes), remember the following:

Each appendix should be clearly labeled—Appendix A, Appendix B.

The source of the chart, graph, whatever, should be given in note form immediately below the material provided.

The Arabic numerals used for pagination in the body of the paper are carried on through end matter such as appendixes as well.

9.2.6. Endnotes (May or may not be necessary)

If you are using parenthetical documentation or if your instructor has asked you to document your sources at the bottom of each page in footnote form, you may ignore this section.

If you are employing endnotes to document your sources, you will need to include those at this point. Adhere to the following guidelines: (See Appendix F for an example.)

- Give your endnotes the simple heading of Notes, centered and positioned approximately one inch from the top of the page.
- All notes should be numbered consecutively, beginning with 1. These numbers, unadorned with punctuation of any kind and slightly raised, should be separated from the notes by a single space.
- If you are using a typewriter, the first line of the note should be indented five spaces. If you are using a word processor, indent the first line approximately three eighths of an inch. Subsequent lines, should they be required, come back to the margin.
- The Arabic numerals used for pagination in the body of the paper are carried on through the documentation.

9.2.7. A bibliography (Almost always required)

Generally speaking, you must include in your paper, immediately following your endnotes (or immediately following the text of your paper if you did not use endnotes), either a complete list of all the sources that you have found useful in writing your paper (even if you have not made direct reference to some of them), or, at the very least, a complete list of the sources that you have actually cited in your paper.

The following format should be employed in providing this list: (See Appendix G for an example.)

- If your list is limited to those sources actually cited in your paper, give it the heading Works Cited. If your list is a broader one, including works beyond those actually cited in your paper, give it the heading Works Consulted. In either case, the heading should appear centered, approximately one inch from the top of the first page of the list.
- Bibliographic entries are not numbered. Instead, they are arranged alphabetically according to the first item in the entry, usually an author's last name.
- The first line of a bibliographic entry starts on the margin. The second line, should there be one, is indented, five spaces if you are using a typewriter; approximately three eighths of an inch if you are using a word processor.
- A series of three hyphens followed by a period should be used in place of an author's name for second and subsequent citations, should an author have more than one work listed in the bibliography.
- The Arabic numerals used for pagination in the body of the paper are carried on through the bibliography.

9.2.8. A back page (Check with your instructor.)

Some teachers appreciate a blank sheet of paper at the back of the research paper because it gives them ample space for comments and suggestions. Such a page also has the advantage of giving the paper tangible, physical closure.

If you do include such a page, do *not* number it.

<u>Notes</u>

Appendix A: Sample Title Page (Traditional Format)

Steroid Abuse Among Olympic Athletes

Sally Goodstudent

Mr. Teachwell

Advanced Composition

15 May 1994

Appendix B: Sample Topic Outline (First Page Only)

Outline

Thesis: The use of anabolic steroids by Olympic athletes has been occurring for a long time; but despite serious steps taken by the International Olympic Committee to discourage such abuse, the battle is far from over.

I.   Background information on steroids

   A. Basic facts

      1. Origin and initial use of steroids

      2. What steroids are

      3. Definitions of <u>androgenic</u> and <u>anabolic</u>

   B. What steroids supposedly do for athletes

      1. Most experts believe steroids increase muscle mass and body weight

      2. Steroids are thought to increase strength and endurance

      3. Steroids may increase aggressiveness and hostility

II. Why some Olympic athletes are tempted to use steroids

   A. Some Olympians feel they need steroids just to compete

   B. Desire to win a strong motive for Olympic athletes to use steroids

      1. Desire to win almost obsessive among some athletes

      2. Dr. Goldman's research on desire to win

      3. Dr. Mirkin's question reveals overwhelming desire to win

   C. Greed an important factor in some Olympians' use of steroids

   D. Pressure from entire world of sports pushes athletes to do "whatever is necessary"

      1. Pressure comes from peers and teammates

      2. Coaches sometimes encourage athletes to use drugs

      3. Fans expect athletes to win at all costs

III. Olympic events most apt to involve the use of steroids

   A. Steroid use among Olympic weightlifters

      1. Olympic weightlifters generally thought to be first to use

      2. Olympic weightlifters believed to be among biggest abusers

      3. Problem so bad among weightlifters some think sport should be eliminated

   B. Other Olympic events involved with steroid abuse

Appendix C: Sample Opening Pages for a Research Paper *Without* a Traditional Title Page (and with Parenthetical Documentation)

Sally Goodstudent

Mr. Teachwell

Advanced Composition

15 May 1994

Steroid Abuse Among Olympic Athletes

When the Canadian sprinter Ben Johnson streaked across the finish line in the 100 meter event in the 1988 summer games, it was a great moment in the history of Olympic track and field. Not only had he convincingly defeated his archrival, the American Carl Lewis, but he had set a new Olympic and world record in the process. Fewer then three days after his spectacular victory, however, Johnson's triumph had turned to disgrace. The gold medal he had so proudly worn on the victory stand had been stripped from him and awarded to Lewis.

The culprit? Anabolic steroids, or 'roids as they are sometimes called by the athletes who use them. Routine tests administered immediately after the race revealed that Johnson was guilty of using this drug so popular among athletes. Unfortunately, Johnson was neither the first not the last Olympian to use this banned substance in the hopes of enhancing athletic performance. Indeed, the use of anabolic steroids by Olympic athletes has been occurring for a long time; but despite serious steps taken by the International Olympic Committee to discourage such abuse, the battle is far from over.

Just what are anabolic steroids, and what do they supposedly do for the athletes who routinely put their health and athletic reputations on the line to use them? Originating in Europe prior to World War II and designed initially as medicines (Dolan 21), steroids are chemical compounds which are either made from or produced synthetically to resemble various human hormones—the chemical agents in the body that trigger specific physiological changes. The steroids preferred by athletes looking for an advantage over their competitors typically imitate the male hormone testosterone—the hormone responsible for such masculine characteristics as facial hair, a deeper voice, a more muscular body, and a generally more aggressive personality (Nardo 19). The full name for these compounds is androgenic-anabolic steroids. The terms androgenic and anabolic derive from the two main effects of testosterone-related steroids, the former referring to the development of male sex characteristics and the latter to the positive impact steroids can have on muscle development and ultimately on body size and strength (Worsnop 513).

Although universal agreement about exactly what steroids do for the athletes who use them does not exist, significant evidence suggests the following: First, because steroids are tailored to imitate testosterone, they can have a significant influence on body weight and muscle mass. For this reason, and because they allow the body to store increased amounts of nitrogen, thus enhancing the development of protein, they can also contribute to substantial increases in strength and endurance (Harris 88). Finally, evidence suggests that steroids sometimes increase aggressiveness and hostility—qualities prized by many athletes.

Needless to say, athletes in many sports and at various levels of competition could be and have been tempted to use drugs that promise the possibility of larger muscles, increased endurance, and a little extra feistiness in the heat of the battle; but Olympic athletes have their own special reasons to be attracted to steroids. Some of them feel that they need the drug just to compete at the high level of competition represented by the Olympic Games. The feeling among some seems to be "'If you don't take it, you won't make it'" (Wicken 48). Indeed, this line of reasoning is apparently what led Ben Johnson to use steroids. As a former Canadian sprinter who knows Johnson has explained, "'He [Johnson] could decide whether to participate at the highest level of sport or not. If he wanted to compete, it was pretty clear steroids were worth one meter at the highest level'" ("Johnson Used Steroids" 46).

Other Olympic athletes turn to steroids out of a simple overwhelming desire to win. The line of reasoning here is that successful athletes are in some ways a self-selecting group and that one of the characteristics that tends to distinguish them is their obsession with winning, even to the point of choosing behaviors potentially dangerous to their very health and well being. In his book <u>Drugs in Sports</u>, Edward Dolan refers to what he calls the "athletic mind-set." As he explains,

> . . . athletes train hard for a single goal or a series of goals. Perhaps the single goal is an Olympic gold medal. Perhaps the series of goals adds up to a string of victories that carry the individual from local to national and then international competitions—or to the ranks of the professionals. Soon, it's all too easy for athletes to think of nothing else. (50)

Just how strong this compulsion can become is illustrated by the research of a couple of doctors close to the world of drugs and sports. One, a Doctor Goldman, reportedly once asked 198 world-class track and field athletes the following question: "'If I had a magic drug that was so fantastic that if you took it once you would win every competition for the next five years, but it had one minor drawback—it would kill you five years after you took it—would you still take the drug?'" Amazingly, over 52 percent of the athletes answered yes (Harris 87). Goldman's findings are paralleled by the research of a Doctor

Mirkin, who reportedly asked 100 runners if they would take a drug guaranteed to help them win Olympic gold knowing that the same drug would end their lives within a year. Again, over 50% of the respondents indicated that they would indeed make the ultimate sacrifice to be an Olympic champion (Dolan 50).

Appendix D: Sample Opening Pages for a Research Paper *With* a Traditional Title Page (Documentation in Footnotes)

Goodstudent 1

When the Canadian sprinter Ben Johnson streaked across the finish line in the 100 meter event in the 1988 summer games, it was a great moment in the history of Olympic track and field. Not only had he convincingly defeated his archrival, the American Carl Lewis, but he had set a new Olympic and world record in the process. Fewer then three days after his spectacular victory, however, Johnson's triumph had turned to disgrace. The gold medal he had so proudly worn on the victory stand had been stripped from him and awarded to Lewis.

The culprit? Anabolic steroids, or 'roids as they are sometimes called by the athletes who use them. Routine tests administered immediately after the race revealed that Johnson was guilty of using this drug so popular among athletes. Unfortunately, Johnson was neither the first not the last Olympian to use this banned substance in the hopes of enhancing athletic performance. Indeed, the use of anabolic steroids by Olympic athletes has been occurring for a long time; but despite serious steps taken by the International Olympic Committee to discourage such abuse, the battle is far from over.

Just what are anabolic steroids, and what do they supposedly do for the athletes who routinely put their health and athletic reputations on the line to use them? Originating in Europe prior to World War II and designed initially as medicines,[1] steroids are chemical compounds which are either made from or produced synthetically to resemble various human hormones—the chemical agents in the body that trigger specific physiological changes. The steroids preferred by athletes looking for an advantage over their competitors typically imitate the male hormone testosterone—the hormone responsible for such masculine characteristics as facial hair, a deeper voice, a more muscular body, and a generally more aggressive personality.[2] The full name for these compounds is androgenic-anabolic steroids. The terms androgenic and anabolic derive from the two main effects of testosterone-related steroids, the former referring to the development of male sex characteristics and the latter to the positive impact steroids can have on muscle development and ultimately on body size and strength.[3]

---

[1] Edward F. Dolan, <u>Drugs in Sports</u>, rev. ed. (New York: Franklin Watts, 1992) 21.

[2] Don Nardo, <u>Drugs and Sports</u> (San Diego: Lucent Books, 1990) 19.

[3] Richard L. Worsnop, "Athletes and Drugs," <u>CQ Researcher</u> 26 July 1991: vol. 1, no. 12, 513, rpt. in <u>Drugs</u> vol. 5 (Boca Raton: Social Issues Resources Series, Inc., 1993) article no. 33.

Although universal agreement about exactly what steroids do for the athletes who use them does not exist, significant evidence suggests the following: First, because steroids are tailored to imitate testosterone, they can have a significant influence on body weight and muscle mass. For this reason, and because they allow the body to store increased amounts of nitrogen, thus enhancing the development of protein, they can also contribute to substantial increases in strength and endurance.[4] Finally, evidence suggests that steroids sometimes increase aggressiveness and hostility—qualities prized by many athletes.

Needless to say, athletes in many sports and at various levels of competition could be and have been tempted to use drugs that promise the possibility of larger muscles, increased endurance, and a little extra feistiness in the heat of the battle; but Olympic athletes have their own special reasons to be attracted to steroids. Some of them feel that they need the drug just to compete at the high level of competition represented by the Olympic Games. The feeling among some seems to be "'If you don't take it, you won't make it.'"[5] Indeed, this line of reasoning is apparently what led Ben Johnson to use steroids. As a former Canadian sprinter who knows Johnson has explained, "'He [Johnson] could decide whether to participate at the highest level of sport or not. If he wanted to compete, it was pretty clear steroids were worth one meter at the highest level.'"[6]

Other Olympic athletes turn to steroids out of a simple overwhelming desire to win. The line of reasoning here is that successful athletes are in some ways a self-selecting group and that one of the characteristics that tends to distinguish them is their obsession with winning, even to the point of choosing behaviors potentially dangerous to their very health and well being. In his book Drugs in Sports, Edward Dolan refers to what he calls the "athletic mind-set." As he explains,

> . . . athletes train hard for a single goal or a series of goals. Perhaps the single goal is an Olympic gold medal. Perhaps the series of goals adds up to a string of victories that carry the individual from local to national and then international competitions—or to the ranks of the professionals. Soon, it's all too easy for athletes to think of nothing else.[7]

Just how strong this compulsion can become is illustrated by the research of a couple of doctors close to the world of drugs and sports. One, a Doctor Goldman, reportedly once

---

[4] Jonathan Harris, Drugged Athletes: Crisis in American Sports (New York: Four Winds, 1987) 88.

[5] Barbara Wicken, "A Deepening Scandal," Macleans 5 June 1989: 48.

[6] "Johnson Used Steroids Seven Years Says Coach," Jet 20 March 1989: 46.

[7] 50.

asked 198 world-class track and field athletes the following question: "'If I had a magic drug that was so fantastic that if you took it once you would win every competition for the next five years, but it had one minor drawback—it would kill you five years after you took it—would you still take the drug?'" Amazingly, over 52 percent of the athletes answered yes.[8] Goldman's findings are paralleled by the research of a Doctor Mirkin, who reportedly asked 100 runners if they would take a drug guaranteed to help them win Olympic gold knowing that the same drug would end their lives within a year. Again, over 50% of the respondents indicated that they would indeed make the ultimate sacrifice to be an Olympic champion.[9]

---

[8] Harris 87.

[9] Dolan 50.

Appendix E: Sample Opening Pages for a Research Paper With a Traditional Title Page (Documentation in Endnotes)

When the Canadian sprinter Ben Johnson streaked across the finish line in the 100 meter event in the 1988 summer games, it was a great moment in the history of Olympic track and field. Not only had he convincingly defeated his archrival, the American Carl Lewis, but he had set a new Olympic and world record in the process. Fewer then three days after his spectacular victory, however, Johnson's triumph had turned to disgrace. The gold medal he had so proudly worn on the victory stand had been stripped from him and awarded to Lewis.

The culprit? Anabolic steroids, or 'roids as they are sometimes called by the athletes who use them. Routine tests administered immediately after the race revealed that Johnson was guilty of using this drug so popular among athletes. Unfortunately, Johnson was neither the first not the last Olympian to use this banned substance in the hopes of enhancing athletic performance. Indeed, the use of anabolic steroids by Olympic athletes has been occurring for a long time; but despite serious steps taken by the International Olympic Committee to discourage such abuse, the battle is far from over.

Just what are anabolic steroids, and what do they supposedly do for the athletes who routinely put their health and athletic reputations on the line to use them? Originating in Europe prior to World War II and designed initially as medicines,[1] steroids are chemical compounds which are either made from or produced synthetically to resemble various human hormones—the chemical agents in the body that trigger specific physiological changes. The steroids preferred by athletes looking for an advantage over their competitors typically imitate the male hormone testosterone—the hormone responsible for such masculine characteristics as facial hair, a deeper voice, a more muscular body, and a generally more aggressive personality.[2] The full name for these compounds is androgenic-anabolic steroids. The terms androgenic and anabolic derive from the two main effects of testosterone-related steroids, the former referring to the development of male sex characteristics and the latter to the positive impact steroids can have on muscle development and ultimately on body size and strength.[3]

Although universal agreement about exactly what steroids do for the athletes who use them does not exist, significant evidence suggests the following: First, because steroids are tailored to imitate testosterone, they can have a significant influence on body weight and muscle mass. For this reason, and because they allow the body to store increased amounts of nitrogen, thus enhancing the development of protein, they can also contribute to substantial increases in strength and endurance.[4] Finally, evidence suggests that steroids sometimes increase aggressiveness and hostility—qualities prized by many athletes.

Needless to say, athletes in many sports and at various levels of competition could be and have been tempted to use drugs that promise the possibility of larger muscles, increased endurance, and a little extra feistiness in the heat of the battle; but Olympic athletes have their own special reasons to be attracted to steroids. Some of them feel that they need the drug just to compete at the high level of competition represented by the Olympic Games. The feeling among some seems to be "'If you don't take it, you won't make it.'"[5] Indeed, this line of reasoning is apparently what led Ben Johnson to use steroids. As a former Canadian sprinter who knows Johnson has explained, "'He [Johnson] could decide whether to participate at the highest level of sport or not. If he wanted to compete, it was pretty clear steroids were worth one meter at the highest level.'"[6]

Other Olympic athletes turn to steroids out of a simple overwhelming desire to win. The line of reasoning here is that successful athletes are in some ways a self-selecting group and that one of the characteristics that tends to distinguish them is their obsession with winning, even to the point of choosing behaviors potentially dangerous to their very health and well being. In his book Drugs in Sports, Edward Dolan refers to what he calls the "athletic mind-set." As he explains,

> . . . athletes train hard for a single goal or a series of goals. Perhaps the single goal is an Olympic gold medal. Perhaps the series of goals adds up to a string of victories that carry the individual from local to national and then international competitions—or to the ranks of the professionals. Soon, it's all too easy for athletes to think of nothing else.[7]

Just how strong this compulsion can become is illustrated by the research of a couple of doctors close to the world of drugs and sports. One, a Doctor Goldman, reportedly once asked 198 world-class track and field athletes the following question: "'If I had a magic drug that was so fantastic that if you took it once you would win every competition for the next five years, but it had one minor drawback—it would kill you five years after you took it—would you still take the drug?'" Amazingly, over 52 percent of the athletes answered yes.[8] Goldman's findings are paralleled by the research of a Doctor Mirkin, who reportedly asked 100 runners if they would take a drug guaranteed to help them win Olympic gold knowing that the same drug would end their lives within a year. Again, over 50% of the respondents indicated that they would indeed make the ultimate sacrifice to be an Olympic champion.[9]

Finally, Olympic athletes are as subject as anyone else to pure and simple greed. Face it, an Olympic medal can be worth big bucks! Hitting pay dirt at the games can turn penniless amateurs into instant millionaires. Nor does one have to win a gold medal to cash in. Within days of winning her silver medal at the 1994 winter games in Lillehammar, Norway, for example, Nancy Kerrigan had signed contracts worth millions with companies as diverse as Revlon and Disney. This is not to suggest, of course, that Kerrigan used steroids; but her financial success as a result of her winning performance at the games illustrates the point—even a silver medal can mean financial security for life. Many Olympians and potential Olympians find the temptation simply too powerful to resist, and they do whatever they think they need to do to win, even to the point of using banned substances such as steroids.

Appendix F: Sample Endnotes (First Page Only)

Notes

[1] Edward F. Dolan, *Drugs in Sports*, rev. ed. (New York: Franklin Watts, 1992) 21.

[2] Don Nardo, *Drugs and Sports* (San Diego: Lucent, 1990) 19.

[3] Richard L. Worsnop, "Athletes and Drugs," CQ Researcher 26 July 1991: 513, rpt. in Drugs vol. 5 (Boca Raton: Social Issues Resources Series, 1993) art. 33.

[4] Jonathan Harris, Drugged Athletes: Crisis in American Sports (New York: Four Winds, 1987) 88.

[5] Barbara Wicken, "A Deepening Scandal," Macleans 5 June 1989: 48.

[6] "Johnson Used Steroids Seven Years Says Coach," Jet 20 March 1989: 46.

[7] 50.

[8] Harris 87.

[9] Dolan 50.

[10] Nardo 25.

[11] Hank Nuwer, Steroids (New York: Franklin Watts, 1990) 53.

[12] Janet Mohan, Drugs, Steroids, and Sports (New York: Franklin Watts) 23.

[13] Nardo 27.

[14] Merrell Noden, "Setting the Records Straight," Sports Illustrated 16 December 1991: 138.

[15] 18.

[16] Lynn Rosellini, John Marks, and Victoria Pope, "The Sports Factories," U.S. News & World Report 17 February 1992: 51.

[17] Nuwer 25.

[18] Lynn Rosellini, Steven Dickman, and Joannie M. Schrof, "Steroid Science: The Molecules of Sport," U.S. News & World Report 17 February 1992: 56.

[19] Dolan 57.

[20] 27.

[21] Jeff Meer, Drugs and Sports (New York: Chelsea House, 1987) 62.

[22] Bill Schiller, "Beating the Drug Rap: Athletes Say Steroid Use is Rampart," Toronto Star 23 July 1988: A1, rpt. in Drugs vol. 4 (Boca Raton: Social Issues Resources Series, 1990) art. 75.

[23] "Olympic Roundup: Austrian Bobsledder Flunks Steroid Test," Seattle Times 15 February 1994, first ed.: C5, Dialog file 707, item 07546058.

Appendix G: Sample Bibliography (First Page of 2)

Works Cited

"Ben Again." Sports Illustrated 15 March 1993: 9.

Dolan, Edward F. Drugs in Sports. Rev. ed. New York: Franklin Watts, 1992.

Harris, Jonathan. Drugged Athletes: Crisis in American Sports. New York: Four Winds, 1987.

Iole, Kevin. "Steroid Use Persists Despite Damning Truth." Las Vegas Review-Journal/
     Sun 28 April 1991: 1E+. Rpt. in Sports Vol. 4. Boca Raton: Social Issues Resources
     Series, 1993. Art. 7.

"Johnson Used Steroids Seven Years Says Coach." Jet 20 March 1989: 46.

Lawrence, Susan V. "Olympics 2000: China's Sporting Dreams." U.S. News & World Report
     17 February 1992: 59.

Lopez, John P. "The Specter of Drugs Still Stalks the Games." Houston Chronicle 7 July
     1992: 1B+. Rpt. in Sports Vol. 4. Boca Raton: Social Issues Resources Series,
     1993. Art. 33.

Meer, Jeff. Drugs & Sports. The Encyclopedia of Psychoactive Drugs, Series 2. Gen.
     ed. Solomon H. Snyder. New York: Chelsea House, 1987.

Mohan, Janet. Drugs, Steroids, and Sports. New York: Franklin Watts, 1988.

Nardo, Don. Drugs and Sports. San Diego: Lucent, 1990.

Noden, Merrell. "Setting the Records Straight." Sports Illustrated 16 December 1991: 138.

Nuwer, Hank. Sports Scandals. Chicago: Franklin Watts, 1994.

---. Steroids. New York: Franklin Watts, 1990.

"Olympic Roundup: Austrian Bobsledder Flunks Steroid Test." Seattle Times 15 February
     1994, first ed.: C5. Dialog file 707, item 07546058.

Reuters, Sharon Robb. "U.S. Coaches Credit China's Rapid Rise to 'Pharmaceutical Warfare.'"
     Seattle Times 5 December 1993, weekend ed.: C12. Dialog file 707, item 07339158.

Rosellini, Lynn, Steven Dickman, and Joannie M. Schrof. "Steroid Science: The Molecules
     of Sport." U.S. News & World Report 17 February 1992: 56-57.

---. John Marks, and Victoria Pope. "The Sports Factories." U.S. News & World Report
     17 February 1992: 48-59.

Schiller, Bill. "Beating the Drug Rap: Athletes Say Steroid Use is Rampant." Toronto
     Star 23 July 1988: A1+. Rpt. in Drugs Vol. 1. Boca Raton: Social Issues Resources
     Series, 1990. Art. 75.

"The Steroid Olympics." The Economist 4-10 July 1992: 81.

Wallace, Bruce. "Victory's Cost." Macleans 2 December 1991: 32.

Notes

Notes

<u>Notes</u>